Unitarian Christianity
and Other Essays

The American Heritage Series

OSKAR PIEST, *General Editor*

[NUMBER TWENTY-ONE]

Unitarian Christianity
and Other Essays

WILLIAM ELLERY CHANNING
Unitarian Christianity and Other Essays

Edited, with an Introduction, by
IRVING H. BARTLETT
Assistant Professor of History
Massachusetts Institute of Technology

A LIBERAL ARTS PRESS BOOK

THE **BOBBS-MERRILL** COMPANY, INC.
A SUBSIDIARY OF HOWARD W. SAMS & CO., INC.
Publishers • INDIANAPOLIS • NEW YORK

CONTENTS

CHRONOLOGY

1780	Born April 7 in Newport, Rhode Island
1794-1798	Undergraduate at Harvard
1798-1800	Tutor in Richmond, Virginia
1800-1801	Theological studies at Newport; influenced by Samuel Hopkins
1802	Theological studies at Harvard; preaches first sermons
1803	Ordained June 1 over Boston's Federal Street Congregation
1813	Begins to play a part in the Unitarian controversy by helping to found *The Christian Disciple*
1814	Marriage to Ruth Gibbs
1815	Defends the "liberal Christians" with the pamphlet *A Letter to the Rev. Samuel C. Thacher . . .*
1819	"Unitarian Christianity"
1820	"The Moral Argument against Calvinism"
1821	"The Evidences of Revealed Religion"
1822-1823	European journey; meets Wordsworth and Coleridge
1828	"Likeness to God"
1830	"Remarks on National Literature"
1830-1831	Trip to Cuba
1832	"Honor Due to All Men"
1835	*Slavery*
1837	Participates in the Elijah Lovejoy meeting at Faneuil Hall
1842	Died October 2 in Bennington, Vermont

INTRODUCTION

Twenty-five years after William Ellery Channing's death, a friend searching after the secret of the man's power was forced to confess that he had been "without learning, without research, not a scholar, not a critic, without imagination or fancy, not a poet, not a word-painter, without humor or wit, without profundity of thought, without grace of elocution." [1]

Yet this was the man who in the eyes of English readers in the second quarter of the nineteenth century ranked with Irving and Cooper as an example of America's literary excellence, the man who was universally acknowledged as the spiritual father of Unitarianism in America, the man whose collected works had run through twenty-two editions twelve years after his death,[2] the man of whom Theodore Parker said: "No man in America has left a sphere of such wide influence, no man since Washington has done so much to elevate his country."[3]

Without being a profound thinker, a great writer, or a man whose actions tipped the scales in a critical moment, Channing left his mark on our history because of his representative influence, because he captured and attempted to synthesize in his living and his thinking the diverse strands of thought which appeared in America at the end of the eighteenth and the beginning of the nineteenth centuries.

In his greatest contribution to American civilization, his work as a minister and religious writer, Channing sought to

---

1 These remarks made at a memorial service for Channing are quoted in David Edgell, *William Ellery Channing: An Intellectual Portrait* (Boston, 1955), p. 104.

2 Robert E. Spiller, "A Case for W. E. Channing," *New England Quarterly* III (1930), 55-81.

3 John Weiss, *Life and Correspondence of Theodore Parker* (New York, 1864), I, 183.

develop an "enlightened" religious faith for the Americans of his generation.

The Enlightenment influenced religious thought in America in at least three different ways. There was first of all the monumental achievement of Jonathan Edwards, who employed his comprehensive knowledge of Newton and Locke to reconstruct and revitalize the central doctrines of Calvinist theology. His *Treatise Concerning Religious Affections* (1746), which sought to provide a scientific explanation for the religious enthusiasms of the Great Awakening, and his essays on freedom of the will and original sin were all intended to show how modern refinements in psychology and physics made meaningful the old doctrines of divine sovereignty, natural depravity, predestination, and supernatural grace. Edwards' impact on religious thought can hardly be overemphasized. In a century dominated by the spirit of skeptics like Voltaire and David Hume, Jonathan Edwards held the line for the great majority of orthodox Protestants in America. In New England, especially, his influence was pervasive, and orthodox ministers were expected to study his works almost as assiduously as the Holy Scriptures.[4]

In the history of American theology in the eighteenth century Jonathan Edwards emerges like a giant among pygmies. His grand statement of Calvinism was intended to be swallowed entire, to provide *the* answer for all doubting believers. After his death in 1758, however, his system became a subject for endless disputation among the Calvinist writers left in his wake. Where Edwards had devoted himself to the great questions of sin, free will, the nature of religious experience, and the sovereignty of God, his followers—rugged, zealous preachers in New England villages for the most part—fell into a pattern of legalistic wrangling over the precise definition of narrow theological concepts.[5] True religion became identified

[4] The two most incisive treatments of Edwards' place in American thought are Clarence Faust and Thomas Johnson, *Jonathan Edwards* (New York, 1935) and Perry Miller, *Jonathan Edwards* (New York, 1949).

[5] Sydney Mead, *Nathaniel William Taylor 1786-1858, A Connecticut Liberal* (Chicago, 1942), pp. 14-16.

with loyalty to a particular system of abstract doctrines, and the attempts to define this loyalty led to prolonged doctrinal disputes, the effects of which were felt in almost every pious household in New England at the turn of the century. "Every child," Harriet Beecher Stowe remembered, "found himself beaten backwards and forwards, like a shuttlecock between the battledores of discussion." [6]

Channing's open-minded, rational approach to religious problems, his distaste for controversy, and his own prejudice against speculative theology can only be understood against the barren history of New England theology after Jonathan Edwards.

Edwards' most famous contemporary, Benjamin Franklin, represents quite a different aspect of the Enlightenment's influence. Franklin, too, was born into a strongly Calvinistic family, and the first money he spent on books went for a collection of John Bunyan's works.[7] Unlike Edwards, however, who was converted and fell in love with the doctrine of divine sovereignty, Franklin was repelled by Calvinist dogma. When he was about fifteen, some volumes attacking deism fell into his hands. "It happened that they wrought an effect on me quite contrary to what was intended by them; for the arguments of the Deists, which were quoted to be refuted, appeared to me much stronger than the refutations; in short, I soon became a thorough Deist." [8] Franklin's new religion, later strengthened by his reading of Locke, Newton, and other Enlightenment writers, emphasized belief in a rational scheme of morality which linked virtue with success, a rational scheme of creation which allowed man to plumb the mysteries of nature by discovering and applying natural laws, and a benevolent God, the prime mover of the universe.

If Jonathan Edwards' achievement was essentially a work of conservation, new tools of thought being used to preserve old

[6] Harriet Beecher Stowe, *Oldtown Folks* (Boston, 1869), p. 376.
[7] Benjamin Franklin, *The Autobiography of Benjamin Franklin* (New York, 1954), p. 16.
[8] *Ibid.*, p. 71.

truths, the speculations of the deists represent the radical influence of the Enlightenment on religion. The genial Franklin, of course, can hardly be called a radical. "He that spits against the Wind," he observed, after reading a particularly outspoken attack on organized religion (perhaps written by Thomas Paine), "spits in his own Face. . . . You might easily display your excellent Talents of reasoning upon a less hazardous subject, and thereby obtain a Rank with our most distinguished authors." [9] Nevertheless, the "Powerful Goodness" whom Franklin addressed every morning before going about his day's business had little in common with the God Edwards worshiped. "The God that holds you over the pit of hell, much as one holds a spider or some loathsome insect over the fire, abhors you and is dreadfully provoked," Edwards once admonished his congregation; "his wrath towards you burns like fire—you are ten thousand times more abominable in his eyes than the most hateful venomous serpent is in ours." [10] And Thomas Paine's blunt assertion that his own mind was his church represents a vision of the dignity of man that Edwards, who taught the virtue of "humility, brokenness of heart and poverty of spirit," would have found incomprehensible.

Channing sympathized with the deists for their courageous reliance on reason and their moral repugnance to Calvinism. Jefferson's remark, that John Calvin's god was really a demon in disguise, he would have understood at once. His own ardently religious nature, however, could never have been satisfied in the chilly contemplation of a first cause instead of a personal God.

The third way in which the Enlightenment influenced religious thought in America lies somewhere between Edwards' conservatism and the deists' radicalism. Deism was never very popular in New England, but there had always been a pronounced reliance upon reason among the Puritans, and as the

9 Frank Luther Mott and Chester Jorgenson, *Benjamin Franklin* (New York, 1936), p. 484.

10 "Sinners in the Hands of an Angry God," in Faust and Johnson, *op. cit.*, p. 164.

eighteenth century unfolded, this rational element in religion was increasingly emphasized by a small, influential group of liberal ministers in the Boston area.

The liberals were distinguished from their orthodox counterparts in the Congregational pulpits of New England by their emphasis on the benevolence of God and the rational elements in man, revelation and nature. They tended to accept the Arminian rather than the Calvinist conception of human nature, which is to say that they believed that man was not predestined to heaven or hell but possessed in himself the capacity for sinful or righteous living. Like the deists, the liberals believed that reason could bring man to a knowledge of religion. Unlike the deists, they believed in a personal God whose word was supernaturally revealed in the Bible and could be verified by reason.

Although the split between the liberals and the orthodox Calvinists ultimately culminated in American Unitarianism, it was a gradual development, beginning from about the time of the Great Awakening (1725). Geography played a definite part, the liberals being strong around Boston and the coastal regions of New England, the Calvinists retaining their strength in the interior, where Jonathan Edwards' influence was particularly powerful. Probably the two most influential liberal ministers were Jonathan Mayhew (1720-1766) and Charles Chauncy (1704-1787), each of whom occupied a position of leadership among the Boston clergy. Mayhew was one of the first prominent New England ministers to challenge the doctrine of the Trinity. Chauncy, who was repelled by the emotionalism which convulsed New England congregations during the Great Awakening, taught that God was a being of rational benevolence, who made man in his own likeness and communicated with him through reason rather than through the affections. In his *Beneficence of the Deity*, published in 1784, the liberal influences of the Enlightenment in American religious thought were beginning to be clearly defined.[11]

11 Conrad Wright's *The Beginnings of Unitarianism in America* (Boston, 1955) contains an excellent analysis of the liberal movement up to 1805.

It was left to William Ellery Channing, four years old when Chauncy's book came out, to provide the liberal tradition with its most classic expression. Born in Newport, Rhode Island, in 1780, Channing was a son of that enlightened generation of American revolutionaries who successfully forced the separation of the colonies from England. His grandfather had signed the Declaration of Independence; his father had been a classmate of James Madison at Princeton. He himself was present as a boy at the convention when Rhode Island ratified the Constitution, and he remembered having met George Washington, who stayed at the Channing house when he visited Newport. In other words, Channing and the new American nation really grew up together, and the optimism, the generous view of human nature on which the American experiment was based, undoubtedly helped to flavor his own thinking.

Channing was a delicate child, sensitive and withdrawn beyond his years. Although not an intellectual prodigy like Jonathan Edwards, his unusual religious sensibility was reflected in the fact that when still a small boy he liked to assemble the other members of his family about him in the form of a congregation and preach to them. Presumably the content of these childhood sermons was Calvinistic, since this was the religious background in which the boy was reared. The Calvinists at this time had split into two groups: the New Calvinists, who followed Jonathan Edwards, and the Old Calvinists, who put preaching before doctrine while attempting to minimize the harsher aspects of the traditional theology. During Channing's youth both parties were represented in Newport. The two most notable ministers in the town were Ezra Stiles, an Old Calvinist who later became president of Yale, and Samuel Hopkins, the most famous of Edwards' disciples. As a boy Channing was greatly impressed by Stiles, in whose personality he found the kind of spirit which ultimately characterized his own career. "In my earliest years," he later wrote, referring to Stiles, "I regarded no human being with equal reverence. . . . [H]is heart was of no sect. He carried into his religion the spirit of liberty, which then stirred the whole country. Intolerance, church tyranny, in all its forms he abhorred. He respected the right of private judgment, where others would have thought themselves authorized to restrain it." [12] Samuel Hopkins' baleful sermons, delivered in a church half ruined by the British during the Revolution, proved less inspiring, and Channing later admitted that "some of the most painful sensations of my childhood were experienced in that comfortless building." [13]

As a well-born New Englander at the end of the eighteenth century, Channing was expected to find his career in either the law or the ministry. By the time he graduated from Harvard in 1798 he felt able to confirm his calling for the ministry. He decided to pursue a course of private study before returning to the Divinity School at Harvard, and to support himself during this period he accepted a position as tutor to a wealthy family in Richmond, Virginia.

The two years spent in Virginia were probably the most crucial in Channing's life, for it was here that he sought to resolve the opposing claims of reason and faith. The problem had been posed for him a few years earlier when he had undergone his first religious experience after reading Francis Hutcheson's work on "divine disinterestedness" [14] ("I longed to die, and felt as if Heaven alone could give room for the exercise of such emotions"[15]). One is led naturally from these words to the account of Jonathan Edwards' conversion a half century earlier. The difference is that Edwards achieved his "sense of the glory of the Divine being" after reading a passage in Timothy on the sovereignty of God, while Channing's was prompted by the work of an eighteenth-century deist. The

[12] W. E. Channing, *Works* (Boston, 1900), p. 423.

[13] William Henry Channing, *The Life of William Ellery Channing, D.D.* (Boston, 1880), p. 15. Referred to hereafter as *Life*.

[14] Francis Hutcheson, influential Scottish philosopher, argued in his *System of Moral Philosophy* (London, 1755) that man has a moral sense and that disinterested acts of benevolence leading to the public good meet with the highest approval from the moral sense.

[15] *Life*, p. 32.

contrast is instructive and points up what became a central task of Channing's life—to make reason and piety walk hand in hand.

Hutcheson did not solve the problem, and at Richmond Channing plunged into a course of reading which he hoped would provide him with a religious assurance that would satisfy his intellect and his heart. He devoured the books of writers like Mary Wollstonecraft, Rousseau, and Godwin—and then bleakly contemplated the fact that these exciting thinkers were all deists who denied the reality of a personal God.[16]

The resulting struggle represents Channing's vigil with the spirit. Refusing to be enticed by the easy ways of the Southern aristocracy which employed him, he began to spend more and more time in study. "Society becomes more and more insipid," he confided to a friend, "I am tired of the fashionable nonsense which dins my ear in every circle, and I am driven to my book and pen for relief and pleasure. . . . I am independent of the world." [17] Sometimes he worked the night through, ignored his diet to an alarming extent, slept on the bare floor in an attempt at self-mortification, and let his wardrobe go until he was ashamed to appear in public.

Ultimately the struggle and the doubts were washed away in a great flood of faith. The man who in later life would frequently declaim against the need for "enthusiasm" in Christian experience, against the undue emphasis Calvinists placed on conversion, was himself converted. "I believe that I never experienced that *change of heart* which is necessary to constitute a Christian," he wrote toward the end of his stay, "till within a few months past. The worldling would laugh at me; he would call conversion a farce. But the man who has felt the influences of the Holy Spirit can oppose fact and experience to empty declaration and contemptuous sneers. You remember the language of the blind man whom Jesus healed,— 'This I know, that whereas I was blind, now I see.' Such is

16 *Life,* p. 57.
17 *Life,* p. 54.

the language which the real Christian may truly utter. Once and not long ago, I was blind, blind to my own condition, blind to the goodness of God, and blind to the love of my Redeemer. Now I behold with shame and confusion the depravity and rottenness of my heart. Now I behold with love and admiration the long suffering and infinite benevolence of Deity." [18]

Channing returned to Newport in 1800 convinced all the more that his future lay in the ministry. While preparing for the Divinity School at Harvard he fell under the influence of Samuel Hopkins, whose preaching had made such an unfavorable impression on him as a boy. Appalled by the older man's pulpit manner ("Such tones never came from any human voice within my hearing"), and revolted by the harsh doctrines which supplied his sermons, Channing still found much to admire in this venerable preacher. The cornerstone of Hopkins' theological system was a belief that holiness consisted in "benevolence or disinterested devotion to the highest good." Since holiness is the character of God, Hopkins argued that evil and sin were introduced into the creation because they were necessary to the highest good. It followed that true virtue was "an entire surrender of personal interest to the benevolent purposes of God." Carried to a logical conclusion, this line of reasoning led to the famous assertion that the true believer should be "willing to be damned for the glory of God." [19]

Hopkins' theology made a lasting impression on Channing. "I am grateful to this stern teacher," he wrote many years later, "for turning my thoughts and heart to the claims and majesty of impartial, universal benevolence." [20] Moreover, the old theologian insisted on living out his principles. Newport had long owed much of its prosperity to the slave trade, but the claim of universal benevolence led Hopkins to defy pub-

18 *Life*, p. 74.
19 W. E. Channing, *Works*, pp. 423-424.
20 *Ibid.*, p. 424.

lic sentiment by attacking slavery and laboring for the improvement of the colored people in Newport long before the abolition movement was organized.

Channing's attitude toward Hopkins is a nice expression of his attitude toward Calvinism. He rejected many doctrines "with a feeling approaching horror," but he admired the old man's sincerity, the vigor which made him seem to be "an illustration of the power of our spiritual nature." Ultimately Hopkins' conception of Christian benevolence, a more spiritualized version of the message he had earlier found in Hutcheson, became the basis of Channing's own moral philosophy.

When Channing returned to Harvard in 1801 to complete his preparation for the ministry, the embattled churches of New England, battered and scarred from generations of theological warfare, were militantly preparing for a new controversy. The struggle between the liberals and the Calvinists had reached an acute stage. Anti-Trinitarian convictions had been expressed at the Episcopal King's Chapel in Boston in 1785, and the Calvinists suspected that what their liberal adversaries really wanted was to introduce the hateful Unitarian heresy into the Congregational pulpits of New England. When the Hollis Professorship of Divinity at Harvard fell vacant in 1803, the way was open for a test of strength between the two parties. With the appointment of the liberal, Henry Ware, to the post in 1805, the "Unitarian controversy" in America can be said to have officially begun. The Calvinists, who for a time at least were able to ignore the differences within their own ranks and make a common front against the enemy, quickly took the offensive. They were able to agree on a merger of several of their periodicals into the *Panoplist*, a journal established to crusade "for the faith once delivered to the saints." Because Harvard was lost to the Unitarians, the Calvinists organized an orthodox seminary of their own at Andover in 1808. Finally the Park Street Church was raised near the corner of Boston Common to enable rugged Calvinist campaigners like Lyman Beecher to carry the battle against the "Boston religion" into the heart of Boston itself.

Channing was ordained as the Congregational minister to Boston's Federal Street Church in 1803. His health had been permanently shattered by the years of travail at Richmond, but the frail figure and pallid complexion he brought to the pulpit were balanced by an intense spirituality in his presence and preaching. Too introspective and too fond of his study to be socially congenial, he impressed everyone with the simplicity of his dress and manners, the clarity and vigor of his preaching.

Channing's theological position during the first ten years of his ministry is not easily defined. Early sermons emphasizing "the *ruins of human nature*" and the vileness of sin indicate that he did not feel estranged from the views of the moderate Calvinists.[21] Indeed, some who knew Channing at this time thought of him more as a disciple of Hopkins than as a Unitarian. The Calvinists, however, did not bother to make subtle distinctions between the various shades of liberalism which infected Boston ministers, and their attacks apparently forced Channing, along with other budding Unitarian ministers, to clarify his position. By 1813, he was ready to help found the *Christian Disciple*, a magazine designed to promote the cause of the Boston liberals. Two years later, when he entered the pamphlet war with a statement distinguishing between the views of English Unitarians and the liberals in America,[22] Channing was recognized as one of the leading Unitarian spokesmen. By now the liberals had begun to assume a stronger position. They had won over a majority of the Congregational churches along the seaboard in New England and were beginning to extend their sphere of influence. It was time for an affirmative statement of their belief. In May 1819, at the ordination of a Unitarian minister in Baltimore, Channing delivered the sermon, "Unitarian Christianity," which not only stated the credo of American Uni-

[21] Edgell, *op. cit.,* p. 24.
[22] W. E. Channing, *A Letter to the Rev. Samuel C. Thacher, on the Aspersions Contained in a Late Number of the Panoplist, on the Ministers of Boston and the Vicinity* (Boston, 1815).

tarians but also became a landmark in America's religious and intellectual history.

The Baltimore sermon indicates the extent to which Channing had succeeded since his years at Richmond in combining rationalism with Christian piety. It is divided into two parts: a statement of the principles which Unitarians use in interpreting Scripture; and an elaboration of some views which they derive from Scripture. So far as the first part is concerned, Channing says simply that reason provides the key to the Bible. "Say what we may, God has given us a rational nature and will call us to account for it." The Bible is a book, written for men in human language, and like all other books it requires of readers "the constant exercise of reason." At this point, and particularly when he asserts "We reason about the Bible precisely as civilians do about the Constitution under which we live," Channing is clearly invoking the spirit of the Enlightenment; Franklin himself might have written the last sentence.

Turning his attention to specific doctrines, Channing asserts in effect that every article of theology must be judged at the bar of reason and moral sense. Unitarians believe in the unity of God and reject the "irrational and unscriptural doctrine of the Trinity." Unitarians believe in the moral perfection of God and reject the Calvinist view of divine sovereignty. "It is not because his will is irresistible, but because his will is the perfection of virtue, that we pay him allegiance. We cannot bow before a being, however great, who governs tyrannically." Since the "unspeakable cruelty" of doctrines like natural depravity and predestination cannot be squared with God's moral perfection, they too are rejected. No arbitrary distinction between saint and sinner is allowable within a morally perfect system; every man must have within himself the capacity for Christian virtue.

The contrast between Channing and Jonathan Edwards could hardly be more complete. Both men experienced a change of heart. But after Edwards' conversion, the doctrines of God's sovereignty, of predestination and natural depravity appeared lovely in his eyes, while Channing insisted that all religious truth must conform to human standards of reason and moral judgment. Still it is easy to make too much of the contrast. Each man responded to the spirit of the Enlightenment in his own way: Edwards employed Locke and Newton to revitalize Calvinist dogma, Channing employed the liberating spirit of eighteenth-century thought to free Christianity from an outmoded theology. The difference between the two men—and this is the important thing—is a difference within Christianity. In other words, Channing was a liberal but not a radical; he was ready to discard old doctrines but he was still an ardent believer.

That Channing's Unitarianism has nothing in it of eighteenth-century skepticism or deism is clearly demonstrated in his discourse on "The Evidences of Revealed Religion" given at Harvard in 1821. Here Channing is attempting to make a rational defense of the miraculous character of Christianity. He traces the growing skepticism toward miracles to the modern conception of the uniformity of nature. The difficulty lies in a mistaken impression that God's power is somehow restrained by natural laws. "We are never to forget that God's adherence to the order of the universe is not necessary and mechanical, but intelligent and voluntary." In other words, Providence still rules the world; God's great moral purpose lies behind the creation, and nature is subject to this purpose if God chooses to communicate with men through miracles. Channing's whole argument seems to be based on the assumption that reason takes us through nature to a God for whom miracles are possible. When he proceeds in this manner, in his rather ineffectual attempts to refute Hume on miracles and in his reliance on Paley, he is making a rational assault on rational skepticism. There is, however, another part to his case for the "evidences" of Christianity, and that is the internal evidence of faith. "I refer to that conviction of the divine original of our religion which springs up and continually gains strength in those who apply it habitually to their tempers and lives, and who imbibe its spirit and hopes. In such men there is a consciousness of the adaptation of Christianity to their noblest faculties—a consciousness of its exalting and consoling influences, of its power to confer the true happiness of human nature, to give that peace which the world cannot give, which assures them that it is not of earthly origin, but a ray from the Everlasting Light, a stream from the Fountain of heavenly wisdom and love."

Thus it is piety as much as reason which dictates the belief in miracles. Like Edwards, who first knows the sense of God's loveliness and then writes *The Treatise on Religious Affections* to show how this knowledge is made possible, Channing also believes before he reasons, and in so doing he attempts to combine the piety of seventeenth-century Americans with the rationalism of their descendants in the early nineteenth century.

Channing's reputation as the outstanding spokesman for American Unitarianism should not be allowed to obscure the fact that he was widely respected during his own lifetime as a man of letters. His fame as a writer rested less on Unitarian sermons than on his "Remarks on National Literature" and his critical essays on Milton, Napoleon, and Fénelon. These were the works best known to his contemporary English readers, among whom he ranked as one of the three or four most significant American writers. He was also widely read on the continent, especially in France. Channing usually appears in anthologies of American literature today as a precursor of the Romantic movement, a pioneer in ideas which New England Transcendentalists like Emerson and Theodore Parker carried to a logical fulfillment. Perhaps his most reprinted piece has been the "Remarks on National Literature" which called for the cultural independence of the American people some seven years before Emerson celebrated the same idea in "The American Scholar."

Whether Channing was, in fact, a Transcendentalist or not is one of those arid subjects over which scholars love to dispute. It is easy to make a case for either point of view. Born in 1780, Channing was of the same generation as the early

Romantic writers, being only a little older than Coleridge and Wordsworth, slightly younger than Cooper, Irving, and Bryant. When Emerson was studying theology at Harvard he made regular pilgrimages to hear Channing's "sublime sermons" and to get special guidance from him for his own reading. Later, when Emerson himself was beginning a career in the pulpit, a parishioner paid him the rare compliment of saying that he promised to be another Channing.[23] Later still, when Emerson had spurned the church as an unnecessary obstruction between man and God and had retired to the "pulpit of the soul," he remembered the difference which Channing had made to the intellectual life of New England. Referring to the beginnings of New England's renaissance, which he dated about 1820 (one year after Channing's "Unitarian Christianity"), Emerson wrote: "We could not then spare a single word he uttered in public, not so much as the reading lesson in Scripture, or a hymn. . . . A poor little invalid all his life, he is yet one of those men who vindicate the power of the American race to produce greatness." [24] As a man and a thinker, then, Channing was profoundly attractive to many of the Transcendentalists. When he died, the grieving Theodore Parker wrote: "Why, oh! my God, are so many left when such are taken. Why could not I have died in his stead?" [25] When one considers these remarks together with the indisputable fact that in some sermons Channing seems to glide almost imperceptibly from a faith in man's reason to the celebration of his divinity ("We see God around us because he dwells within us. . . . In truth, the beauty and glory of God's works are revealed to the mind by a light beaming from itself"), the case for Channing as a Transcendentalist appears plausible enough.

But the other side to the question is that Channing apparently never thought of himself as a Transcendentalist. To-

[23] Ralph Rusk, *The Life of Ralph Waldo Emerson* (New York, 1949), pp. 101, 103, 139.

[24] Ralph Waldo Emerson, *Lectures and Biographical Sketches* (Boston, 1904), p. 339.

[25] Weiss, *op. cit.*, I, 183.

ward the end of his life he wrote to a friend that he had never been able to develop an enthusiasm for the "new views" in religion. "I seem to *learn* very little. Their vague generalities do not satisfy me. They seem wholly to overlook the actual moral condition of the human race on which Christianity is founded." [26] When Theodore Parker delivered his notorious "Discourse of the Transient and Permanent in Christianity" in 1841 and rejected the necessity for scriptural revelation in favor of an "Absolute Religion" of human consciousness, Channing was not impressed. He had not changed his own ideas on revelation since "The Evidences of Revealed Religion" twenty years earlier, and Parker's rejection of the miraculous element in Christianity offended him. "Without miracles the historical Christ is gone," he wrote after reading Parker's sermon. "No such being is left us; and in losing him how much is lost! Reduce Christianity to a set of abstract ideas, sever it from its teacher, and it ceases to be 'the power of God unto salvation.' " [27] Still, the man who had insisted in 1819 that Unitarianism was a faith for liberals had no sympathy now with those of his brother ministers who sought to muzzle Parker for fear that his radical views would damage their denomination. Channing's liberalism was too ingrained for this. "Let the full heart pour itself forth!" he wrote, referring to Parker; "I think he is probably to be one of the many who are made wise by error and suffering. *But I honor his virtues.*" [28]

The point at which the Enlightenment becomes transformed into that phase of Romanticism which we know as New England Transcendentalism is not easily distinguished. The change is subtle, essentially a change in emphasis—from the admiration of nature as the rational handiwork of God to the love of nature as an incarnation of God, from the conviction that reasonable men can chart their own destiny in the world to

26 Elizabeth Peabody, *Reminiscences of William Ellery Channing, D.D.* (Boston, 1880), p. 430.

27 *Ibid.*, p. 424.

28 *Ibid.*, p. 429.

Emerson's rapturous realization that "within man is the soul of the whole." The significance of Channing is that he spans the gap between the two periods. Like Rousseau, he has one foot planted squarely in the Enlightenment, the other in the nineteenth century, and he faces toward the future.

The Romantic in Channing is clearly apparent in his attitude toward sentiment as opposed to reason and in his feeling toward nature. "What a writer!" he exclaimed after reading *Eloise*. "Rousseau is the only French author I have ever read who knows the way to the heart. . . ." [29] Nature also knew the way to the heart, and even as a boy Channing was aware that the feelings which she aroused in him were at one with his religious impulses. "No spot on earth has helped to form me so much as that beach," he once said of a favorite retreat in Newport. "There in reverential sympathy with the mighty power around me, I became conscious of a power within. . . ." [30] And in Virginia, too preoccupied to enjoy the society of others, he sought inspiration along the luxuriant banks of the James River. "I snuff up the fresh breezes; I throw myself on the soft bed of grass which nature has formed for her favorites; I feel every power within me renewed and invigorated." [31]

Perhaps he would never have resorted to Emerson's extravagance in likening himself to "a transparent eyeball," but Channing would certainly have satisfied Emerson's definition that "the lover of nature is he whose inward and outward senses are still truly adjusted to each other; who has retained the spirit of infancy even into the era of manhood." [32] This sympathy between the two men is also observed in the fact that they were both warm admirers of Wordsworth and Coleridge, both seeking out the two great Romantic poets during their separate trips to England.

Channing, however, was too much a product of the Enlight-

[29] *Life,* p. 57.
[30] *Life,* p. 79.
[31] *Life,* p. 59.
[32] Ralph Waldo Emerson, *Nature Addresses and Lectures* (Boston, 1883), p. 14.

enment to put exclusive reliance on feeling. Looking back on his youth, he once remarked that his whole life had been a struggle with his feelings. Goldsmith and Southey had moved him to tears, but no good resulted from such outbursts. It was not the Romantic writers but the liberal Scottish philosophers, whom he first read as an undergraduate at Harvard, who showed Channing the way out of this dilemma.[33] He found from reading Francis Hutcheson and Adam Ferguson that man has a natural capacity to pursue what is good, and through reason can naturally triumph over the evil in nature and in himself. He also read Richard Price, who, he claimed, "saved me from Locke's philosophy" by demonstrating that the mind was not limited to sense experience but could, through reason, know moral ideas directly.[34] Torn between the imperatives of reason and feeling, Channing finally saw the light. "A cloud of error burst from my mind. I found that virtue did not consist in feelings, but in *acting from a sense of duty*." [35]

The lengths to which Channing was taken by the knowledge that every man can know his duty is clearly observed in one of his most eloquent sermons, "Likeness to God." The essential point of the sermon is that there is in the mind of every man an essential likeness to God, and it is his duty to enhance this likeness. As man draws closer to God he becomes more and more aware of the divine presence everywhere, espe-

[33] The "Scottish School" of philosophy founded by Thomas Reid (1710-1796) was a reaction against the skeptical conclusions of David Hume. These "common-sense" philosophers, studied extensively by American college students during the early nineteenth century, sought to make moral philosophy dependent on the facts of consciousness rather than on sense experience. For Channing the significant Scottish philosophers were Adam Ferguson (1723-1816), whose *Principles of Moral and Political Science* was published in 1792, and Richard Price (1723-1791), whose *Review of the Principal Questions in Morals* came out in 1787. For a good summary of the Scottish philosophy see James McCosh, *The Scottish Philosophy* (New York, 1880), pp. 1-11. For its impact on America see Woodbridge Riley, *American Thought* (New York, 1923), pp. 118-120.

[34] *Life*, p. 34.

[35] *Life*, p. 61.

cially within himself. The proof of the doctrine can be found in human consciousness. Man comes to know God not simply by reading Scripture, or by reasoning that nature must have a supernatural source—man finds God by looking into his own mind. "That unbounded spiritual energy which we call God is conceived by us only through consciousness, through the knowledge of ourselves." The gulf between the infinite God and finite man has been overemphasized. "There are traces of infinity in the human mind." In all its higher actions the soul has "a character of infinity." If man participates in divinity, a new kind of preaching is demanded. Sin is now properly considered as "the ruin of God's noblest work" and "Christ's greatness is manifested in the greatness of the nature which he was sent to redeem."

Despite the fact that Channing's debt is to the Scottish philosophers rather than to Kant, the transcendental overtones in this sermon cannot be ignored. It was delivered in 1828, eight years before Emerson's *Nature,* ten years before the *Divinity School Address.* Yet the similarity between Channing's conception of the divine potential in human nature and Emerson's assertion, "If a man is at heart just, then in so far is he God," [36] is unmistakable.

In the final analysis, Channing's greatest contribution to American letters must be found in the fact, as Van Wyck Brooks has said, that he was the "great awakener" for New England.[37] The path to Transcendentalism lay through Unitarianism, and it was Channing who redeemed the sons and daughters of Puritanism from an oppressive, outmoded dogmatism that they might properly celebrate the possibilities of human nature and all created things.

Glancing through the titles of those of Channing's addresses included in the volume of his collected works, one is struck by the variety of causes which the man espoused:

[36] Emerson, *Nature Addresses and Lectures,* p. 122.
[37] Van Wyck Brooks, *The Flowering of New England* (New York, 1936), p. 109.

"Self Culture," "On the Elevation of the Laboring Classes," "Ministry for the Poor," "Address on Temperance," "Remarks on Associations," "Lecture on War," "Remarks on the Slavery Question." The list is a veritable catalogue of the reform projects which laid claim to the enthusiasm of Americans during the first part of the nineteenth century.

Channing's interest in social reform had several roots. The gospel of disinterested benevolence which had led Samuel Hopkins to pen one of the first antislavery tracts in America was undoubtedly influential. The Scottish philosophers, with their strong emphasis on the moral imperatives in every man, also pointed the way to reform. Finally, Channing, born in the afterglow of revolutionary enthusiasm, growing up almost with the Declaration of Independence, was influenced by the humanitarian spirit of the Enlightenment.

One thing is certain, and that is that Channing did not inherit his liberalism. Any child born into the Newport aristocracy in 1780 was bound to have Federalist blood in his veins, and he was no exception. As an undergraduate at Harvard he was conservative in politics and, like the other well-bred Harvard men, took the respectable line that the French Revolution was the chief menace to civilization in the eighteenth century. At Richmond, however, under the influence of deist writers like Godwin and Rousseau, freshly imbued with the insight that man has "a spark of divinity in his bosom," Channing was converted to socialism. "You must convince mankind," he wrote to a friend, "that they themselves and all which they possess, are but *parts of a great whole*, that they are bound by God, their common Father, to *labor* for the good of this great whole; that their wants are but few, and can easily be supplied; . . . You profess to believe in the Christian religion. Does not Christianity favor such a scheme? I believe it will be hard to reconcile Christian humility, charity, and contempt of riches with the present establishment of human affairs." [38]

[38] *Life*, p. 65.

Although this radical position made his New England friends suspect that Channing had been seduced by the Jacobins in Virginia, it did not prevail for long. In matters of reform as in theology, Channing was essentially liberal rather than radical. His liberalism and participation in reform causes were directly consequent on his religious beliefs. The two fundamental ideas which thread their way through all of Channing's writing are faith in the parental character of God and belief in the dignity of man. The sermon "Unitarian Christianity" is no more than an elaboration of these two ideas. The dignity of man is confirmed by the rational faculties with which he must test the truth of revelation. And the parental character of God is the basis for Channing's moral argument against Calvinism: the Father who loves his children will never condemn them for sins they cannot help or arbitrarily favor one child at the expense of another. Again in "The Evidences of Christianity" Channing says that the objections against miracles "will lose their weight just in proportion as we strengthen our conviction of God's power over nature and of his parental interest in his creatures—There is something like coldness and repulsiveness in instructing us only by fixed, inflexible laws of nature." And in the third selection in this book it is precisely the likeness between father and child that Channing equates with man's relationship to God.

How the two central ideas in Channing's thought fuse together to provide the ideological basis for his humanitarianism can be observed in the sermon "Honor Due to All Men." A great blessing of Christianity, Channing says, is "the new relation it establishes between man and man" by recognizing the common greatness in human nature. This greatness is found in man's sense of duty. "It is this moral power which makes all men essentially equal, which annihilates all the distinctions of this world." He who obeys the moral command within shows honor to all men. The ferment of reform which seethed not only in America but throughout the Western world in the 1830s and 1840s seemed to Channing to be the result of this principle and to foreshadow the coming of a golden age. "I see the dawning of that great principle, that the individual is not made to be the instrument of others, but to govern himself by an inward law, and to advance toward his proper perfection."

The previous quotation suggests that the mature Channing never completely abandoned the utopianism of his youth; the inference is reinforced when we note his attendance at Boston's famous Convention of the Friends of Universal Reform in 1840. A little paper in Hingham captured the spirit of that kind of occasion. "Since the day of Pentecost, we don't believe such a conglomeration of strange tongues has ever been known. All sorts of things were said by all sorts of persons on all sorts of subjects. Clergymen were there as well as laymen, Trinitarians and Unitarians, Transcendentalists and Latterists, Universalists and Calvinists, Methodists and Baptists, Atheists and Deists, Mormons and Socialists, white men and black men, men with beards and men without, no-money men and anti-property men, Cape Cod Come-outers and Latter Day Saints, Jews and Quakers, Dialists and Plain Speakers, Unionists and Perfectionists, Non Resistants, Abolitionists, Women Lecturers, Owenites, Grahamites, and all the Ists and Ites, the contented and discontented *ons* and *ans* that make up this queer compound called the world." [39]

These colorful reformers were the people who kept the pot boiling. Channing was not one of them really. In the first place, he was too austere. In the second place, he was an aristocrat who sometimes allowed a note of paternalism to creep into his voice when talking about the poor.[40] Moreover, he disliked radicalism and controversy. It would have been alien to his temperament, for example, to have been at Gar-

---

[39] Quoted in the *Liberator* (Boston), November 5, 1841. The quotation does not refer to the meeting Channing attended but to a similar meeting held the following year. It captures the spirit, however, which characterized most of the reform congresses during the period.

[40] See for example the opening paragraphs of his "Ministry for the Poor," *Works*, pp. 73 ff.

rison's side when the latter so horrified proper Bostonians with
the first trumpet blasts of the *Liberator*. On the other hand,
nothing is more typical of Channing's liberalism than his attitude toward slavery and the abolitionists. Although he had
strongly opposed slavery ever since he had observed it in
Virginia, and although Garrison personally tried to get him
to support his movement, Channing stopped short of the extremes to which the abolitionists were led in their denunciation of the evil. His hesitancy may have been partly due to
the fact that he had known good people during his youth in
Newport who had tolerated slavery, but it was primarily because he feared extremes of any kind. After a trip to Cuba
for his health in 1830 which convinced him all the more of the
evils of slavery, he was more prepared to speak out on the subject. His pamphlet *Slavery* which appeared in 1835 was ex-
tremely influential, coming as it did not from an obscure
radical but from a man of acknowledged influence and pres-
tige. Two years later, when the abolitionists were denied the
use of Faneuil Hall to honor the memory of Elijah Lovejoy,
who had just been killed protecting his antislavery press from
a proslavery mob in Alton, Illinois, it was Channing who used
his influence to get the necessary permission from the city
commissioners. Free speech was on trial in Boston and Channing was on the side of freedom.

In his insistence that religious faith be made manifest in
good works, Channing probably did as much as any other
American of his generation to unite the forces of religion
and humanitarianism. His contribution to our history was
great, but his reward at the hands of his contemporaries
served only to prove that the liberal who insists on honoring
all men is bound to earn the hatred of some. Before he spoke
out on the slavery issue, Channing was damned by the abolitionists for his silence. After he spoke out, they said he had
not gone far enough. But in the eyes of Beacon Street and in
the eyes of the substantial businessmen in Boston he had gone
too far. He was cut by his own parishioners. When one of his
dearest friends, the abolitionist Charles Follen, was drowned

at sea, the congregation denied Channing's request that the Massachusetts Antislavery Society hold a commemoration service in the church. It was primarily because of this coldness that Channing refused further salary from the Federal Street Church and lived in partial retirement during his last years.[41]

Channing lived from 1780 to 1842. His reputation as a representative figure, a symbol of the intellectual and social forces at work in America during this period, is secure. His influence in the development of American civilization has been lasting. Without being an exciting writer like Emerson or Thoreau, he did as much as any single man to prepare the way for one of the richest and most unique movements in our literature. Without being an agitator like Garrison or Wendell Phillips, capable of goading, taunting, jeering an indifferent populace to action, he preached the gospel of human dignity which nourished the unrelenting reformers before the Civil War. Without being a rigorous theologian like Jonathan Edwards, he pointed the liberal direction which Protestant thinkers in America would pursue for over a century.

IRVING H. BARTLETT

41 Edgell, *op. cit.*, p. 43.

SELECTED BIBLIOGRAPHY

CHANNING'S WORKS

Channing's Notebook: Passages from the Unpublished Manuscripts of William Ellery Channing. Edited by Grace Ellery Channing. Boston, 1887.

The Works of William E. Channing, D.D. Boston, 1900.

COLLATERAL READING

Channing, William Henry. *The Life of William Ellery Channing, D.D.* Boston, 1880.

Edgell, David P. *William Ellery Channing: An Intellectual Portrait.* Boston, 1955.

Ladu, Arthur I. "Channing and Transcendentalism," *American Literature,* XI (1939), 129-137.

Peabody, Elizabeth. *Reminiscences of Rev. Wm. Ellery Channing, D.D.* Boston, 1880.

Schneider, Herbert W. "The Intellectual Background of William Ellery Channing," *Church History,* VII (1938), 3-23.

Spiller, Robert E. "A Case for W. E. Channing," *New England Quarterly,* III (1930), 55-81.

Wright, Conrad. *The Beginnings of Unitarianism in America.* Boston, 1955.

NOTE ON THE TEXT

The five essays included in the present volume are taken from the 1886 edition of *The Works of William E. Channing, D. D.* published in Boston by the American Unitarian Association. The punctuation has been modified, and in occasional instances the spelling modernized, to conform to current preferred usage. Footnotes are the editor's.

I. H. B.

Unitarian Christianity
and Other Essays

UNITARIAN CHRISTIANITY

Discourse at the Ordination of the Rev. Jared Sparks,
Baltimore, 1819.

1 Thess. v. 21: "Prove all things; hold fast
that which is good."

The peculiar circumstances of this occasion not only justify but seem to demand a departure from the course generally followed by preachers at the introduction of a brother into the sacred office. It is usual to speak of the nature, design, duties, and advantages of the Christian ministry; and on these topics I should now be happy to insist, did I not remember that a minister is to be given this day to a religious society whose peculiarities of opinion have drawn upon them much remark, and, may I not add, much reproach. Many good minds, many sincere Christians, I am aware, are apprehensive that the solemnities of this day are to give a degree of influence to principles which they deem false and injurious. The fears and anxieties of such men I respect; and, believing that they are grounded in part on mistake, I have thought it my duty to lay before you, as clearly as I can, some of the distinguishing opinions of that class of Christians in our country who are known to sympathize with this religious society. I must ask your patience, for such a subject is not to be dispatched in a narrow compass. I must also ask you to remember that it is impossible to exhibit in a single discourse our views of every doctrine of revelation, much less the differences of opinion which are known to subsist among ourselves. I shall confine myself to topics on which our sentiments have been misrepresented or which distinguish us most widely from others. May I not hope to be heard with candor? God deliver us all from prejudice and unkindness, and fill us with the love of truth and virtue!

There are two natural divisions under which my thoughts will be arranged. I shall endeavor to unfold, 1st, the principles which we adopt in interpreting the Scriptures; and 2dly, some of the doctrines which the Scriptures, so interpreted, seem to us clearly to express.

I. We regard the Scriptures as the records of God's successive revelations to mankind, and particularly of the last and most perfect revelation of his will by Jesus Christ. Whatever doctrines seem to us to be clearly taught in the Scriptures, we receive without reserve or exception. We do not, however, attach equal importance to all the books in this collection. Our religion, we believe, lies chiefly in the New Testament. The dispensation of Moses, compared with that of Jesus, we consider as adapted to the childhood of the human race, a preparation for a nobler system, and chiefly useful now as serving to confirm and illustrate the Christian Scriptures. Jesus Christ is the only master of Christians, and whatever he taught, either during his personal ministry or by his inspired Apostles, we regard as of divine authority and profess to make the rule of our lives.

This authority which we give to the Scriptures is a reason, we conceive, for studying them with peculiar care and for inquiring anxiously into the principles of interpretation by which their true meaning may be ascertained. The principles adopted by the class of Christians in whose name I speak need to be explained because they are often misunderstood. We are particularly accused of making an unwarrantable use of reason in the interpretation of Scripture. We are said to exalt reason above revelation, to prefer our own wisdom to God's. Loose and undefined charges of this kind are circulated so freely that we think it due to ourselves, and to the cause of truth, to express our views with some particularity.

Our leading principle in interpreting Scripture is this, that the Bible is a book written for men, in the language of men, and that its meaning is to be sought in the same manner as that of other books. We believe that God, when He speaks to the human race, conforms, if we may so say, to the established rules of speaking and writing. How else would the Scriptures avail us more than if communicated in an unknown tongue?

Now all books and all conversation require in the reader or hearer the constant exercise of reason; or their true import is only to be obtained by continual comparison and inference. Human language, you well know, admits various interpretations; and every word and every sentence must be modified and explained according to the subject which is discussed, according to the purposes, feelings, circumstances, and principles of the writer, and according to the genius and idioms of the language which he uses. These are acknowledged principles in the interpretation of human writings; and a man whose words we should explain without reference to these principles would reproach us justly with a criminal want of candor and an intention of obscuring or distorting his meaning.

Were the Bible written in a language and style of its own, did it consist of words which admit but a single sense and of sentences wholly detached from each other, there would be no place for the principles now laid down. We could not reason about it as about other writings. But such a book would be of little worth; and perhaps, of all books, the Scriptures correspond least to this description. The word of God bears the stamp of the same hand which we see in his works. It has infinite connections and dependences. Every proposition is linked with others, and is to be compared with others, that its full and precise import may be understood. Nothing stands alone. The New Testament is built on the Old. The Christian dispensation is a continuation of the Jewish, the completion of a vast scheme of providence requiring great extent of view in the reader. Still more, the Bible treats of subjects on which we receive ideas from other sources besides itself—such subjects as the nature, passions, relations, and duties of man—and it expects us to restrain and modify its language by the known truths which observation and experience furnish on these topics.

We profess not to know a book which demands a more frequent exercise of reason than the Bible. In addition to the remarks now made on its infinite connections, we may observe that its style nowhere affects the precision of science or the accuracy of definition. Its language is singularly glowing, bold, and figurative, demanding more frequent departures from the literal sense than that of our own age and country, and consequently demanding more continual exercise of judgment. We find, too, that the different portions of this book, instead of being confined to general truths, refer perpetually to the times when they were written, to states of society, to modes of thinking, to controversies in the church, to feelings and usages which have passed away, and without the knowledge of which we are constantly in danger of extending to all times and places what was of temporary and local application. We find, too, that some of these books are strongly marked by the genius and character of their respective writers, that the Holy Spirit did not so guide the Apostles as to suspend the peculiarities of their minds, and that a knowledge of their feelings, and of the influences under which they were placed, is one of the preparations for understanding their writings. With these views of the Bible, we feel it our bounden duty to exercise our reason upon it perpetually, to compare, to infer, to look beyond the letter to the spirit, to seek in the nature of the subject and the aim of the writer his true meaning; and, in general, to make use of what is known for explaining what is difficult and for discovering new truths.

Need I descend to particulars to prove that the Scriptures demand the exercise of reason? Take, for example, the style in which they generally speak of God, and observe how habitually they apply to him human passions and organs. Recollect the declarations of Christ: that he came not to send peace but a sword; that unless we eat his flesh and drink his blood we have no life in us; that we must hate father and mother, and pluck out the right eye; and a vast number of passages equally bold and unlimited. Recollect the unqualified manner in which it is said of Christians that they possess all things, know all things, and can do all things. Recollect the verbal contradiction between Paul and James, and the apparent clashing of some parts of Paul's writings with the general doctrines and end of Christianity. I might extend the enumeration indefinitely; and who does not see that we must limit all these passages by the known attributes of God, of Jesus Christ, and of human nature, and by the circumstances under which they were written, so as to give the language a quite different import from what it would require had it been applied to different beings, or used in different connections.

Enough has been said to show in what sense we make use of reason in interpreting Scripture. From a variety of possible interpretations we select that which accords with the nature of the subject and the state of the writer, with the connection of the passage, with the general strain of Scripture, with the known character and will of God, and with the obvious and acknowledged laws of nature. In other words, we believe that God never contradicts in one part of Scripture what He teaches in another; and never contradicts in revelation what He teaches in his works and providence. And we therefore distrust every interpretation which, after deliberate attention, seems repugnant to any established truth. We reason about the Bible precisely as civilians do about the constitution under which we live; who, you know, are accustomed to limit one provision of that venerable instrument by others, and to fix the precise import of its parts by inquiring into its general spirit, into the intentions of its authors, and into the prevalent feelings, impressions, and circumstances of the time when it was framed. Without these principles of interpretation, we frankly acknowledge that we cannot defend the divine authority of the Scriptures. Deny us this latitude, and we must abandon this book to its enemies.

We do not announce these principles as original or peculiar to ourselves. All Christians occasionally adopt them, not excepting those who most vehemently decry them when they happen to menace some favorite article of their creed. All Christians are compelled to use them in their controversies with infidels. All sects employ them in their warfare with one another. All willingly avail themselves of reason when it can be pressed into the service of their own party, and only complain of it when its weapons wound themselves. None reason more frequently than those from whom we differ. It is astonishing what a fabric they rear from a few slight hints about the fall of our first parents; and how ingeniously they extract from detached passages mysterious doctrines about the divine nature. We do not blame them for reasoning so abundantly but for violating the fundamental rules of reasoning, for sacrificing the plain to the obscure and the general strain of Scripture to a scanty number of insulated texts.

We object strongly to the contemptuous manner in which human reason is often spoken of by our adversaries because it leads, we believe, to universal skepticism. If reason be so dreadfully darkened by the fall that its most decisive judgments on religion are unworthy of trust, then Christianity, and even natural theology, must be abandoned; for the existence and veracity of God, and the divine original of Christianity, are conclusions of reason and must stand or fall with it. If revelation be at war with this faculty, it subverts itself, for the great question of its truth is left by God to be decided at the bar of reason. It is worthy of remark how nearly the bigot and the skeptic approach. Both would annihilate our confidence in our faculties, and both throw doubt and confusion over every truth. We honor revelation too highly to make it the antagonist of reason or to believe that it calls us to renounce our highest powers.

We indeed grant that the use of reason in religion is accompanied with danger. But we ask any honest man to look back on the history of the church and say whether the renunciation of it be not still more dangerous. Besides, it is a plain fact that men reason as erroneously on all subjects as on religion. Who does not know the wild and groundless theories which have been framed in physical and political science? But who ever supposed that we must cease to exercise reason on nature and society because men have erred for ages in explaining them? We grant that the passions continually, and sometimes fatally, disturb the rational faculty in its inquiries into revelation. The ambitious contrive to find doctrines in the Bible which favor their love of dominion. The timid and dejected discover there a gloomy system, and the mystical and fanatical a visionary theology. The vicious can find examples or assertions on which to build the hope of a late repentance or of acceptance on easy terms. The falsely refined contrive to light on doctrines which have not been soiled by vulgar handling. But the passions do not distract the reason in religious any more than in other inquiries which excite strong and general interest; and this faculty, of consequence, is not to be renounced in religion unless we are prepared to discard it universally. The true inference from the almost endless errors which have darkened theology is, not that we are to neglect and disparage our powers, but to exert them more patiently, circumspectly, uprightly—the worst errors, after all, having sprung up in that church which proscribes reason and demands from its members implicit faith. The most pernicious doctrines have been the growth of the darkest times, when the general credulity encouraged bad men and enthusiasts to broach their dreams and inventions and to stifle the faint remonstrances of reason by the menaces of everlasting perdition. Say what we may, God has given us a rational nature and will call us to account for it. We may let it sleep, but we do so at our peril. Revelation is addressed to us as rational beings. We may wish, in our sloth, that God had given us a system demanding no labor of comparing, limiting, and inferring. But such a system would be at variance with the whole character of our present existence; and it is the part of wisdom to take revelation as it is given to us, and to interpret it by the help of the faculties which it everywhere supposes and on which it is founded.

To the views now given an objection is commonly urged from the character of God. We are told that, God being infinitely wiser than men, his discoveries will surpass human reason. In a revelation from such a teacher we ought to expect propositions which we cannot reconcile with one another, and which may seem to contradict established truths; and it becomes us not to question or explain them away, but to believe and adore, and to submit our weak and carnal reason to the divine word. To this objection we have two short answers. We say, first, that it is impossible that a teacher of infinite wisdom should expose those whom he would teach to infinite error. But if once we admit that propositions which in their literal sense appear plainly repugnant to one another, or to any known truth, are still to be literally understood and received, what possible limit can we set to the belief of contradictions? What shelter have we from the wildest fanaticism, which can always quote passages that, in their literal and obvious sense, give support to its extravagances? How can the Protestant escape from transubstantiation, a doctrine most clearly taught us, if the submission of reason, now contended for, be a duty? How can we even hold fast the truth of revelation; for if one apparent contradiction may be true, so may another, and the proposition that Christianity is false, though involving inconsistency, may still be a verity?

We answer again that, if God be infinitely wise, He cannot sport with the understandings of his creatures. A wise teacher discovers his wisdom in adapting himself to the capacities of his pupils, not in perplexing them with what is unintelligible, not in distressing them with apparent contradictions, not in filling them with a skeptical distrust of their own powers. An infinitely wise teacher, who knows the precise extent of our minds and the best method of enlightening them, will surpass all other instructors in bringing down truth to our apprehension, and in showing its loveliness and harmony. We ought, indeed, to expect occasional obscurity in such a book as the Bible, which was written for past and future ages as well as for the present. But God's wisdom is a pledge that whatever is necessary for *us*, and necessary for salvation, is revealed too plainly to be mistaken, and too consistently to be questioned, by a sound and upright mind. It is not the mark of wisdom to use an unintelligible phraseology, to communicate what is above our capacities, to confuse and unsettle the intellect by appearances of contradiction. We honor our Heavenly Teacher too much to ascribe to him such a revelation. A revelation is a gift of light. It cannot thicken our darkness and multiply our perplexities.

II. Having thus stated the principles according to which we interpret Scripture, I now proceed to the second great head of this discourse, which is to state some of the views which we derive from that sacred book, particularly those which distinguish us from other Christians.

1. In the first place, we believe in the doctrine of God's UNITY, or that there is one God and one only. To this truth we give infinite importance, and we feel ourselves bound to take heed lest any man spoil us of it by vain philosophy. The proposition that there is one God seems to us exceedingly plain. We understand by it that there is one being, one mind, one person, one intelligent agent, and one only, to whom underived and infinite perfection and dominion belong. We conceive that these words could have conveyed no other meaning to the simple and uncultivated people who were set apart to be the depositaries of this great truth and who were utterly incapable of understanding those hairbreadth distinctions between being and person which the sagacity of later ages has discovered. We find no intimation that this language was to be taken in an unusual sense, or that God's unity was a quite different thing from the oneness of other intelligent beings.

We object to the doctrine of the Trinity that, while acknowledging in words, it subverts in effect the unity of God. According to this doctrine, there are three infinite and equal persons possessing supreme divinity, called the Father, Son, and Holy Ghost. Each of these persons, as described by theologians, has his own particular consciousness, will, and perceptions. They love each other, converse with each other, and delight in each other's society. They perform different parts in man's redemption, each having his appropriate office and neither doing the work of the other. The Son is mediator, and not the Father. The Father sends the Son, and is not himself sent; nor is He conscious, like the Son, of taking flesh. Here, then, we have three intelligent agents, possessed of different consciousnesses, different wills, and different perceptions, performing different acts and sustaining different relations; and if these things do not imply and constitute three minds or beings, we are utterly at a loss to know how three minds or beings are to be formed. It is difference of properties and acts and consciousness which leads us to the belief of different intelligent beings, and, if this mark fails us, our whole knowledge falls; we have no proof that all the agents and persons in the universe are not one and the same mind. When we attempt to conceive of three Gods, we can do nothing more than represent to ourselves three agents, distinguished from each other by similar marks and peculiarities to those which separate the persons of the Trinity; and when common Christians hear these persons spoken of as conversing with each other, loving each other, and performing different acts, how can they help regarding them as different beings, different minds?

We do, then, with all earnestness, though without reproaching our brethren, protest against the irrational and unscriptural doctrine of the Trinity. "To us," as to the Apostle and the primitive Christians, "there is one God, even the Father." With Jesus, we worship the Father as the only living and true God. We are astonished that any man can read the New Testament and avoid the conviction that the Father alone is God. We hear our Saviour continually appropriating this character to the Father. We find the Father continually distinguished from Jesus by this title. "God sent his Son." "God anointed Jesus." Now, how singular and inexplicable is this phraseology, which fills the New Testament, if this title belong equally to Jesus, and if a principal object of this book is to reveal him as God, as partaking equally with the Father in supreme divinity! We challenge our opponents to adduce one passage in the New Testament where the word God means three persons, where it is not limited to one person, and where, unless turned from its usual sense by the connection, it does not mean the Father. Can stronger proof be given that the doctrine of three persons in the Godhead is not a fundamental doctrine of Christianity?

This doctrine, were it true, must, from its difficulty, singularity, and importance, have been laid down with great clearness, guarded with great care, and stated with all possible precision. But where does this statement appear? From the many passages which treat of God, we ask for one, one only, in which we are told that He is a threefold being, or that He is three persons, or that He is Father, Son, and Holy Ghost. On the contrary, in the New Testament, where, at least, we might expect many express assertions of this nature, God is declared to be one, without the least attempt to prevent the acceptation of the words in their common sense; and He is always spoken of and addressed in the singular number, that is, in language which was universally understood to intend a single person, and to which no other idea could have been attached without an express admonition. So entirely do the Scriptures abstain from stating the Trinity that when our opponents would insert it into their creeds and doxologies they are compelled to leave the Bible and to invent forms of words altogether unsanctioned by Scriptural phraseology. That a doctrine so strange, so liable to misapprehension, so fundamental as this is said to be, and requiring such careful exposition should be left so undefined and unprotected, to be made out by inference, and to be hunted through distant and detached parts of Scripture—this is a difficulty which, we think, no ingenuity can explain.

We have another difficulty. Christianity, it must be remembered, was planted and grew up amidst sharp-sighted enemies who overlooked no objectionable part of the system and who must have fastened with great earnestness on a doctrine involving such apparent contradictions as the Trinity. We cannot conceive an opinion against which the Jews, who prided themselves on an adherence to God's unity, would have raised an equal clamor. Now, how happens it that in the apostolic writings, which relate so much to objections against Christianity and to the controversies which grew out of this religion, not one word is said implying that objections were brought against the gospel from the doctrine of the Trinity, not one word is uttered in its defense and explanation, not a word to rescue it from reproach and mistake? This argument has almost the force of demonstration. We are persuaded that, had three divine persons been announced by the first preachers of Christianity, all equal and all infinite, one of whom was the very Jesus who had lately died on the cross, this peculiarity of Christianity would have almost absorbed every other, and the great labor of the Apostles would have been to repel the continual assaults which it would have awakened. But the fact is that not a whisper of objection to Christianity on that account reaches our ears from the apostolic age. In the Epistles we see not a trace of controversy called forth by the Trinity.

We have further objections to this doctrine, drawn from its practical influence. We regard it as unfavorable to devotion, by dividing and distracting the mind in its communion with God. It is a great excellence of the doctrine of God's unity, that it offers to us ONE OBJECT of supreme homage, adoration, and love, One Infinite Father, one Being of beings, one original and fountain, to whom we may refer all good, in whom all our powers and affections may be concentrated, and whose lovely and venerable nature may pervade all our thoughts. True piety, when directed to an undivided Deity, has a chasteness, a singleness, most favorable to religious awe and love. Now, the Trinity sets before us three distinct objects of supreme adoration; three infinite persons, having equal claims on our hearts; three divine agents, performing different offices and to be acknowledged and worshiped in different relations. And is it possible, we ask, that the weak and limited mind of man can attach itself to these with the same power and joy as to One Infinite Father, the only First Cause, in whom all the blessings of nature and redemption meet as their center and source? Must not devotion be distracted by the equal and rival claims of three equal persons, and must not the worship of the conscientious, consistent Christian be disturbed by an apprehension lest he withhold from one or another of these his due proportion of homage!

We also think that the doctrine of the Trinity injures devotion, not only by joining to the Father other objects of worship, but by taking from the Father the supreme affection which is his due and transferring it to the Son. This is a most important view. That Jesus Christ, if exalted into the infinite Divinity, should be more interesting than the Father, is precisely what might be expected from history and from the principles of human nature. Men want an object of worship like themselves, and the great secret of idolatry lies in this propensity. A God clothed in our form and feeling our wants and sorrows speaks to our weak nature more strongly than a Father in heaven, a pure spirit, invisible and unapproachable save by the reflecting and purified mind. We think, too, that the peculiar offices ascribed to Jesus by the popular theology make him the most attractive person in the Godhead. The Father is the depositary of the justice, the vindicator of the rights, the avenger of the laws of the Divinity. On the other hand, the Son, the brightness of the divine mercy, stands between the incensed Deity and guilty humanity, exposes his meek head to the storms and his compassionate breast to the sword of the divine justice, bears our whole load of punishment, and purchases with his blood every blessing which descends from heaven. Need we state the effect of these representations, especially on common minds, for whom Christianity was chiefly designed and whom it seeks to bring to the Father as the loveliest being? We do believe that the worship of a bleeding, suffering God tends strongly to absorb the mind and to draw it from other objects, just as the human tenderness of the Virgin Mary has given her so conspicuous a place in the devotions of the Church of Rome. We believe, too, that this worship, though attractive, is not most fitted to spiritualize the mind, that it awakens human transport rather than that deep veneration of the moral perfections of God which is the essence of piety.

2. Having thus given our views of the unity of God, I pro-

ceed, in the second place, to observe that we believe in the unity of Jesus Christ. We believe that Jesus is one mind, one soul, one being, as truly one as we are, and equally distinct from the one God. We complain of the doctrine of the Trinity that, not satisfied with making God three beings, it makes Jesus Christ two beings, and thus introduces infinite confusion into our conceptions of his character. This corruption of Christianity, alike repugnant to common sense and to the general strain of Scripture, is a remarkable proof of the power of a false philosophy in disfiguring the simple truth of Jesus.

According to this doctrine, Jesus Christ, instead of being one mind, one conscious, intelligent principle whom we can understand, consists of two souls, two minds; the one divine, the other human; the one weak, the other almighty; the one ignorant, the other omniscient. Now we maintain that this is to make Christ two beings. To denominate him one person, one being, and yet to suppose him made up of two minds, infinitely different from each other, is to abuse and confound language and to throw darkness over all our conceptions of intelligent natures. According to the common doctrine, each of these two minds in Christ has its own consciousness, its own will, its own perceptions. They have, in fact, no common properties. The divine mind feels none of the wants and sorrows of the human, and the human is infinitely removed from the perfection and happiness of the divine. Can you conceive of two beings in the universe more distinct? We have always thought that one person was constituted and distinguished by one consciousness. The doctrine that one and the same person should have two consciousnesses, two wills, two souls, infinitely different from each other, this we think an enormous tax on human credulity.

We say that if a doctrine so strange, so difficult, so remote from all the previous conceptions of men be indeed a part, and an essential part, of revelation, it must be taught with great distinctness, and we ask our brethren to point to some plain, direct passage where Christ is said to be composed of two minds infinitely different yet constituting one person. We find none. Other Christians, indeed, tell us that this doctrine is necessary to the harmony of the Scriptures, that some texts ascribe to Jesus Christ human, and others divine properties, and that to reconcile these we must suppose two minds, to which these properties may be referred. In other words, for the purpose of reconciling certain difficult passages, which a just criticism can in a great degree, if not wholly, explain, we must invent a hypothesis vastly more difficult, and involving gross absurdity. We are to find our way out of a labyrinth by a clue which conducts us into mazes infinitely more inextricable.

Surely, if Jesus Christ felt that he consisted of two minds, and that this was a leading feature of his religion, his phraseology respecting himself would have been colored by this peculiarity. The universal language of men is framed upon the idea that one person is one person, is one mind and one soul; and when the multitude heard this language from the lips of Jesus, they must have taken it in its usual sense, and must have referred to a single soul all which he spoke, unless expressly instructed to interpret it differently. But where do we find this instruction? Where do you meet, in the New Testament, the phraseology which abounds in Trinitarian books and which necessarily grows from the doctrine of two natures in Jesus? Where does this divine teacher say, "This I speak as God, and this as man; this is true only of my human mind, this only of my divine"? Where do we find in the Epistles a trace of this strange phraseology? Nowhere. It was not needed in that day. It was demanded by the errors of a later age.

We believe, then, that Christ is one mind, one being, and, I add, a being distinct from the one God. That Christ is not the one God, not the same being with the Father, is a necessary inference from our former head, in which we saw that the doctrine of three persons in God is a fiction. But on so important a subject I would add a few remarks. We wish that those from whom we differ would weigh one striking fact. Jesus, in his preaching, continually spoke of God. The word was always in his mouth. We ask, does he by this word ever mean himself? We say, never. On the contrary, he most plainly distinguishes between God and himself, and so do his disciples. How this is to be reconciled with the idea that the manifestation of Christ as God was a primary object of Christianity, our adversaries must determine.

If we examine the passages in which Jesus is distinguished from God, we shall see that they not only speak of him as another being, but seem to labor to express his inferiority. He is continually spoken of as the Son of God, sent of God, receiving all his powers from God, working miracles because God was with him, judging justly because God taught him, having claims on our belief because he was anointed and sealed by God, and as able of himself to do nothing. The New Testament is filled with this language. Now we ask what impression this language was fitted and intended to make? Could any who heard it have imagined that Jesus was the very God to whom he was so industriously declared to be inferior; the very Being by whom he was sent, and from whom he professed to have received his message and power? Let it here be remembered that the human birth, and bodily form, and humble circumstances, and mortal sufferings of Jesus must all have prepared men to interpret, in the most unqualified manner, the language in which his inferiority to God was declared. Why, then, was this language used so continually, and without limitation, if Jesus were the Supreme Deity, and if this truth were an essential part of his religion? I repeat it, the human condition and sufferings of Christ tended strongly to exclude from men's minds the idea of his proper Godhead; and, of course, we should expect to find in the New Testament perpetual care and effort to counteract this tendency, to hold him forth as the same being with his Father, if this doctrine were, as is pretended, the soul and center of his religion. We should expect to find the phraseology of Scripture cast into the mold of this doctrine, to hear familiarly of God the Son, of our Lord God Jesus, and to be told that to us there is one God, even Jesus. But, instead of this, the inferiority of Christ pervades the New Testament. It is not only implied in the general phraseology, but repeatedly and decidedly expressed, and unaccompanied with any admonition to prevent its application to his whole nature. Could it, then, have been the great design of the sacred writers to exhibit Jesus as the Supreme God?

I am aware that these remarks will be met by two or three texts in which Christ is called God, and by a class of passages, not very numerous, in which divine properties are said to be ascribed to him. To these we offer one plain answer. We say that it is one of the most established and obvious principles of criticism that language is to be explained according to the known properties of the subject to which it is applied. Every man knows that the same words convey very different ideas when used in relation to different beings. Thus, Solomon *built* the temple in a different manner from the architect whom he employed; and God *repents* differently from man. Now we maintain that the known properties and circumstances of Christ, his birth, sufferings, and death, his constant habit of speaking of God as a distinct being from himself, his praying to God, his ascribing to God all his power and offices—these acknowledged properties of Christ, we say, oblige us to interpret the comparatively few passages which are thought to make him the Supreme God in a manner consistent with his distinct and inferior nature. It is our duty to explain such texts by the rule which we apply to other texts in which human beings are called gods and are said to be partakers of the divine nature, to know and possess all things and to be filled with all God's fullness. These latter passages we do not hesitate to modify and restrain and turn from the most obvious sense, because this sense is opposed to the known properties of the beings to whom they relate; and we maintain that we adhere to the same principle, and use no greater latitude, in explaining as we do the passages which are thought to support the Godhead of Christ.

Trinitarians profess to derive some important advantages from their mode of viewing Christ. It furnishes them, they tell us, with an infinite atonement, for it shows them an infinite being suffering for their sins. The confidence with which this fallacy is repeated astonishes us. When pressed with the question whether they really believe that the infinite and unchangeable God suffered and died on the cross, they acknowledge that this is not true, but that Christ's human mind alone sustained the pains of death. How have we, then, an infinite sufferer? This language seems to us an imposition on common minds, and very derogatory to God's justice, as if this attribute could be satisfied by a sophism and a fiction.

We are also told that Christ is a more interesting object, that his love and mercy are more felt, when he is viewed as the Supreme God who left his glory to take humanity and to suffer for men. That Trinitarians are strongly moved by this representation we do not mean to deny; but we think their emotions altogether founded on a misapprehension of their own doctrines. They talk of the second person of the Trinity's leaving his glory and his Father's bosom to visit and save the world. But this second person, being the unchangeable and infinite God, was evidently incapable of parting with the least degree of his perfection and felicity. At the moment of his taking flesh, he was as intimately present with his Father as before, and equally with his Father filled heaven, and earth, and immensity. This Trinitarians acknowledge; and still they profess to be touched and overwhelmed by the amazing humiliation of this immutable being! But not only does their doctrine, when fully explained, reduce Christ's humiliation to a fiction, it almost wholly destroys the impressions with which his cross ought to be viewed. According to their doctrine, Christ was comparatively no sufferer at all. It is true, his human mind suffered; but this, they tell us, was an infinitely small part of Jesus, bearing no more proportion to his whole nature than a single hair of our heads to the whole body, or than a drop to the ocean. The divine mind of Christ, that which was most properly himself, was infinitely happy at the very moment of the suffering of his humanity. While hanging on the cross, he was the happiest being in the universe, as happy as the infinite Father; so that his pains, compared with his felicity, were nothing. This Trinitarians do, and must, acknowledge. It follows necessarily from the immutableness of the divine nature which they ascribe to Christ; so that their system, justly viewed, robs his death of interest, weakens our sympathy with his sufferings, and is, of all others, most unfavorable to a love of Christ founded on a sense of his sacrifices for mankind. We esteem our own views to be vastly more affecting. It is our belief that Christ's humiliation was real and entire, that the whole Saviour, and not a part of him, suffered, that his crucifixion was a scene of deep and unmixed agony. As we stand round his cross, our minds are not distracted, nor our sensibility weakened, by contemplating him as composed of incongruous and infinitely differing minds, and as having a balance of infinite felicity. We recognize in the dying Jesus but one mind. This, we think, renders his sufferings, and his patience and love in bearing them, incomparably more impressive and affecting than the system we oppose.

3. Having thus given our belief on two great points, namely, that there is one God, and that Jesus Christ is a being distinct from and inferior to God, I now proceed to another point on which we lay still greater stress. We believe in the *moral perfection of God*. We consider no part of theology so important as that which treats of God's moral character; and we value our views of Christianity chiefly as they assert his amiable and venerable attributes.

It may be said that in regard to this subject all Christians agree, that all ascribe to the Supreme Being infinite justice, goodness, and holiness. We reply that it is very possible to speak of God magnificently and to think of him meanly; to apply to his person high-sounding epithets, and to his government principles which make him odious. The Heathens called Jupiter the greatest and the best; but his history was black with cruelty and lust. We cannot judge of men's real ideas of God by their general language, for in all ages they have hoped to soothe the Deity by adulation. We must inquire into their particular views of his purposes, of the principles of his administration, and of his disposition toward his creatures.

We conceive that Christians have generally leaned toward a very injurious view of the Supreme Being. They have too often felt as if He were raised, by his greatness and sovereignty, above the principles of morality, above those eternal laws of equity and rectitude to which all other beings are subjected. We believe that in no being is the sense of right so strong, so omnipotent, as in God. We believe that his almighty power is entirely submitted to his perceptions of rectitude; and this is the ground of our piety. It is not because He is our Creator merely, but because He created us for good and holy purposes; it is not because his will is irresistible but because his will is the perfection of virtue that we pay him allegiance. We cannot bow before a being, however great and powerful, who governs tyrannically. We respect nothing but excellence, whether on earth or in heaven. We venerate not the loftiness of God's throne, but the equity and goodness in which it is established.

We believe that God is infinitely good, kind, benevolent, in the proper sense of these words—good in disposition as well as in act; good not to a few, but to all; good to every individual, as well as to the general system.

We believe, too, that God is just; but we never forget that his justice is the justice of a good being, dwelling in the same mind and acting in harmony with perfect benevolence. By this attribute we understand God's infinite regard to virtue or moral worth expressed in a moral government; that is, in giving excellent and equitable laws, and in conferring such rewards, and inflicting such punishments, as are best fitted to secure their observance. God's justice has for its end the highest virtue of the creation, and it punishes for this end alone; and thus it coincides with benevolence; for virtue and happiness, though not the same, are inseparably conjoined.

God's justice, thus viewed, appears to us to be in perfect harmony with his mercy. According to the prevalent systems of theology, these attributes are so discordant and jarring that to reconcile them is the hardest task and the most wonderful achievement of infinite wisdom. To us they seem to be intimate friends, always at peace, breathing the same spirit, and seeking the same end. By God's mercy, we understand not a blind instinctive compassion, which forgives without reflection and without regard to the interests of virtue. This, we acknowledge, would be incompatible with justice and also with enlightened benevolence. God's mercy, as we understand it, desires strongly the happiness of the guilty—but only through their penitence. It has a regard to character as truly as his justice. It defers punishment, and suffers long, that the sinner may return to his duty, but leaves the impenitent and unyielding to the fearful retribution threatened in God's word.

To give our views of God in one word, we believe in his parental character. We ascribe to him not only the name but the dispositions and principles of a father. We believe that He has a father's concern for his creatures, a father's desire for their improvement, a father's equity in proportioning his commands to their powers, a father's joy in their progress, a father's readiness to receive the penitent, and a father's justice for the incorrigible. We look upon this world as a place of education in which He is training men by prosperity and adversity, by aids and obstructions, by conflicts of reason and passion, by motives to duty and temptations to sin, by a various discipline suited to free and moral beings for union with himself and for a sublime and ever-growing virtue in heaven.

Now, we object to the systems of religion which prevail among us that they are adverse, in a greater or less degree, to these purifying, comforting, and honorable views of God; that they take from us our Father in heaven, and substitute for him a being whom we cannot love if we would, and whom we ought not to love if we could. We object, particularly on this ground, to that system which arrogates to itself the name of Orthodoxy and which is now industriously propagated through our country. This system, indeed, takes various shapes, but in all it casts dishonor on the Creator. According to its old and genuine form, it teaches that God brings us into life wholly depraved, so that under the innocent features of our childhood is hidden a nature averse to all good and propense to all evil, a nature which exposes us to God's displeasure and wrath even before we have acquired power to understand our duties or to reflect upon our actions. According to a more modern exposition, it teaches that we came from the hands of our Maker with such a constitution, and are placed under such influences and circumstances, as to render certain and infallible the total depravity of every human being from the first moment of his moral agency; and it also teaches that the offense of the child, who brings into life this ceaseless tendency to unmingled crime, exposes him to the sentence of everlasting damnation. Now, according to the plainest principles of morality, we maintain that a natural constitution of the mind, unfailingly disposing it to evil, and to evil alone, would absolve it from guilt; that to give existence under this condition would argue unspeakable cruelty; and that to punish the sin of this unhappily constituted child with endless ruin would be a wrong unparalleled by the most merciless despotism.

This system also teaches that God selects from this corrupt mass a number to be saved, and plucks them, by a special influence, from the common ruin; that the rest of mankind, though left without that special grace which their conversion requires, are commanded to repent, under penalty of aggravated woe; and that forgiveness is promised them on terms which their very constitution infallibly disposes them to reject, and in rejecting which they awfully enhance the punishments of hell. These proffers of forgiveness and exhortations of amendment, to beings born under a blighting curse, fill our minds with a horror which we want words to express.

That this religious system does not produce all the effects on character which might be anticipated, we most joyfully admit. It is often, very often, counteracted by nature, conscience, common sense, by the general strain of Scripture, by the mild example and precepts of Christ, and by the many positive declarations of God's universal kindness and perfect equity. But still we think that we see its unhappy influence. It tends to discourage the timid, to give excuses to the bad, to feed the vanity of the fanatical, and to offer shelter to the bad feelings of the malignant. By shocking, as it does, the fundamental principles of morality, and by exhibiting a severe and partial Deity, it tends strongly to pervert the moral faculty, to form a gloomy, forbidding, and servile religion, and to lead men to substitute censoriousness, bitterness, and persecution for a tender and impartial charity. We think, too, that this system, which begins with degrading human nature, may be expected to end in pride; for pride grows out of a consciousness of high distinctions, however obtained, and no distinction is so great as that which is made between the elected and abandoned of God.

The false and dishonorable views of God which have now been stated we feel ourselves bound to resist unceasingly. Other errors we can pass over with comparative indifference. But we ask our opponents to leave to us a GOD worthy of our love and trust, in whom our moral sentiments may delight, in whom our weaknesses and sorrows may find refuge. We cling to the divine perfections. We meet them everywhere in creation, we read them in the Scriptures, we see a lovely image of them in Jesus Christ; and gratitude, love, and veneration call on us to assert them. Reproached as we often are by men, it is our consolation and happiness that one of our chief offenses is the zeal with which we vindicate the dishonored goodness and rectitude of God.

4. Having thus spoken of the unity of God, of the unity of Jesus and his inferiority to God, and of the perfections of the divine character, I now proceed to give our views of the mediation of Christ and of the purposes of his mission. With regard to the great object which Jesus came to accomplish, there seems to be no possibility of mistake. We believe that he was sent by the Father to effect a moral or spiritual deliverance of mankind; that is, to rescue men from sin and its consequences, and to bring them to a state of everlasting purity and happiness. We believe, too, that he accomplishes this sublime purpose by a variety of methods—by his instructions respecting

God's unity, parental character, and moral government, which are admirably fitted to reclaim the world from idolatry and impiety to the knowledge, love, and obedience of the Creator; by his promises of pardon to the penitent, and of divine assistance to those who labor for progress in moral excellence; by the light which he has thrown on the path of duty; by his own spotless example, in which the loveliness and sublimity of virtue shine forth to warm and quicken as well as guide us to perfection; by his threatenings against incorrigible guilt; by his glorious discoveries of immortality; by his sufferings and death; by that signal event, the resurrection, which powerfully bore witness to his divine mission, and brought down to men's senses a future life; by his continual intercession, which obtains for us spiritual aid and blessings; and by the power with which he is invested of raising the dead, judging the world, and conferring the everlasting rewards promised to the faithful.

We have no desire to conceal the fact that a difference of opinion exists among us in regard to an interesting part of Christ's mediation—I mean, in regard to the precise influence of his death on our forgiveness. Many suppose that this event contributes to our pardon, as it was a principal means of confirming his religion and of giving it a power over the mind; in other words, that it procures forgiveness by leading to that repentance and virtue which is the great and only condition on which forgiveness is bestowed. Many of us are dissatisfied with this explanation, and think that the Scriptures ascribe the remission of sins to Christ's death with an emphasis so peculiar that we ought to consider this event as having a special influence in removing punishment, though the Scriptures may not reveal the way in which it contributes to this end.

Whilst, however, we differ in explaining the connection between Christ's death and human forgiveness—a connection which we all gratefully acknowledge—we agree in rejecting many sentiments which prevail in regard to his mediation. The idea which is conveyed to common minds by the popular system that Christ's death has an influence in making God placable or merciful, in awakening his kindness toward men, we reject with strong disapprobation. We are happy to find that this very dishonorable notion is disowned by intelligent Christians of that class from which we differ. We recollect, however, that, not long ago, it was common to hear of Christ as having died to appease God's wrath, and to pay the debt of sinners to his inflexible justice; and we have a strong persuasion that the language of popular religious books, and the common mode of stating the doctrine of Christ's mediation, still communicate very degrading views of God's character. They give to multitudes the impression that the death of Jesus produces a change in the mind of God toward man, and that in this its efficacy chiefly consists. No error seems to us more pernicious. We can endure no shade over the pure goodness of God. We earnestly maintain that Jesus, instead of calling forth, in any way or degree, the mercy of the Father, was sent by that mercy to be our Saviour; that he is nothing to the human race but what he is by God's appointment; that he communicates nothing but what God empowers him to bestow; that our Father in heaven is originally, essentially, and eternally placable and disposed to forgive; and that his unborrowed, underived, and unchangeable love is the only fountain of what flows to us through his Son. We conceive that Jesus is dishonored, not glorified, by ascribing to him an influence which clouds the splendor of divine benevolence.

We further agree in rejecting, as unscriptural and absurd, the explanation given by the popular system of the manner in which Christ's death procures forgiveness for men. This system used to teach as its fundamental principle that man, having sinned against an infinite Being, has contracted infinite guilt, and is consequently exposed to an infinite penalty. We believe, however, that this reasoning, if reasoning it may be called, which overlooks the obvious maxim that the guilt of a being must be proportioned to his nature and powers, has fallen into disuse. Still the system teaches that sin, of whatever degree, exposes to endless punishment, and that the whole human race, being infallibly involved by their nature in sin, owe this awful penalty to the justice of their Creator. It teaches that this penalty cannot be remitted, in consistency with the honor of the divine law, unless a substitute be found to endure it or to suffer an equivalent. It also teaches that, from the nature of the case, no substitute is adequate to this work save the infinite God himself; and accordingly, God, in his second person, took on him human nature that He might pay to his own justice the debt of punishment incurred by men and might thus reconcile forgiveness with the claims and threatenings of his law. Such is the prevalent system. Now, to us, this doctrine seems to carry on its front strong marks of absurdity; and we maintain that Christianity ought not to be encumbered with it unless it be laid down in the New Testament fully and expressly. We ask our adversaries, then, to point to some plain passages where it is taught. We ask for one text in which we are told that God took human nature that He might make an infinite satisfaction to his own justice; for one text which tells us that human guilt requires an infinite substitute; that Christ's sufferings owe their efficacy to their being borne by an infinite being; or that his divine nature gives infinite value to the sufferings of the human. Not *one word* of this description can we find in the Scriptures; not a text which even hints at these strange doctrines. They are altogether, we believe, the fictions of theologians. Christianity is in no degree responsible for them. We are astonished at their prevalence. What can be plainer than that God cannot in any sense be a sufferer or bear a penalty in the room of his creatures? How dishonorable to him is the supposition that his justice is now so severe as to exact infinite punishment for the sins of frail and feeble men, and now so easy and yielding as to accept the limited pains of Christ's human soul as a full equivalent for the endless woes due from the world? How plain is it also, according to this doctrine, that God, instead of being plenteous in forgiveness, never forgives; for it seems absurd to speak of men as forgiven when their whole punishment, or an equivalent to it, is borne by a substitute? A scheme more fitted to obscure the brightness of Christianity and the mercy of God, or less suited to give comfort to a guilty and troubled mind, could not, we think, be easily framed.

We believe, too, that this system is unfavorable to the character. It naturally leads men to think that Christ came to change God's mind rather than their own; that the highest object of his mission was to avert punishment rather than to communicate holiness; and that a large part of religion consists in disparaging good works and human virtue for the purpose of magnifying the value of Christ's vicarious sufferings. In this way a sense of the infinite importance and indispensable necessity of personal improvement is weakened, and high-sounding praises of Christ's cross seem often to be substituted for obedience to his precepts. For ourselves, we have not so learned Jesus. While we gratefully acknowledge that he came to rescue us from punishment, we believe that he was sent on a still nobler errand, namely, to deliver us from sin itself, and to form us to a sublime and heavenly virtue. We regard him as a Saviour chiefly as he is the light, physician, and guide of the dark, diseased, and wandering mind. No influence in the universe seems to us so glorious as that over the character; and no redemption so worthy of thankfulness as the restoration of the soul to purity. Without this, pardon, were it possible, would be of little value. Why pluck the sinner from hell, if a hell be left to burn in his own breast? Why raise him to heaven, if he remain a stranger to its sanctity and love? With these impressions, we are accustomed to value the gospel chiefly as it abounds in effectual aids, motives, excitements to a generous and divine virtue. In this virtue, as in a common center, we see all its doctrines, precepts, promises meet; and we believe that faith in this religion is of no worth, and contributes nothing to salvation, any further than as it uses these doctrines, precepts, promises, and the whole life, character, sufferings, and triumphs of Jesus as the means of purifying the mind, of changing it into the likeness of his celestial excellence.

5. Having thus stated our views of the highest object of Christ's mission, that it is the recovery of men to virtue or

holiness, I shall now, in the last place, give our views of the nature of Christian virtue, or true holiness. We believe that all virtue has its foundation in the moral nature of man, that is, in conscience or his sense of duty, and in the power of forming his temper and life according to conscience. We believe that these moral faculties are the grounds of responsibility and the highest distinctions of human nature, and that no act is praiseworthy any further than it springs from their exertion. We believe that no dispositions infused into us without our own moral activity are of the nature of virtue, and therefore we reject the doctrine of irresistible divine influence on the human mind, molding it into goodness as marble is hewn into a statue. Such goodness, if this word may be used, would not be the object of moral approbation any more than the instinctive affections of inferior animals or the constitutional amiableness of human beings.

By these remarks, we do not mean to deny the importance of God's aid or Spirit; but by his Spirit we mean a moral, illuminating, and persuasive influence, not physical, not compulsory, not involving a necessity of virtue. We object, strongly, to the idea of many Christians respecting man's impotence and God's irresistible agency on the heart, believing that they subvert our responsibility and the laws of our moral nature, that they make men machines, that they cast on God the blame of all evil deeds, that they discourage good minds and inflate the fanatical with wild conceits of immediate and sensible inspiration.

Among the virtues, we give the first place to the love of God. We believe that this principle is the true end and happiness of our being, that we were made for union with our Creator, that his infinite perfection is the only sufficient object and true resting place for the insatiable desires and unlimited capacities of the human mind, and that, without him, our noblest sentiments, admiration, veneration, hope, and love would wither and decay. We believe, too, that the love of God is not only essential to happiness, but to the strength and perfection of all the virtues; that conscience, without the sanction of God's authority and retributive justice, would be a weak director; that benevolence, unless nourished by communion with his goodness, and encouraged by his smile, could not thrive amidst the selfishness and thanklessness of the world; and that self-government, without a sense of the divine inspection, would hardly extend beyond an outward and partial purity. God, as He is essentially goodness, holiness, justice, and virtue, so He is the life, motive, and sustainer of virtue in the human soul.

But while we earnestly inculcate the love of God, we believe that great care is necessary to distinguish it from counterfeits. We think that much which is called piety is worthless. Many have fallen into the error that there can be no excess in feelings which have God for their object; and, distrusting as coldness that self-possession without which virtue and devotion lose all their dignity, they have abandoned themselves to extravagances which have brought contempt on piety. Most certainly, if the love of God be that which often bears its name, the less we have of it the better. If religion be the shipwreck of understanding, we cannot keep too far from it. On this subject we always speak plainly. We cannot sacrifice our reason to the reputation of zeal. We owe it to truth and religion to maintain that fanaticism, partial insanity, sudden impressions, and ungovernable transports are anything rather than piety.

We conceive that the true love of God is a moral sentiment, founded on a clear perception and consisting in a high esteem and veneration of his moral perfections. Thus it perfectly coincides, and is, in fact, the same thing, with the love of virtue, rectitude, and goodness. You will easily judge, then, what we esteem the surest and only decisive signs of piety. We lay no stress on strong excitements. We esteem him, and him only, a pious man who practically conforms to God's moral perfections and government; who shows his delight in God's benevolence by loving and serving his neighbor; his delight in God's justice by being resolutely upright; his sense of God's purity by regulating his thoughts, imagination, and desires; and whose conversation, business, and domestic life are swayed by a regard to God's presence and authority. In all things else men may deceive themselves. Disordered nerves may give them strange sights, and sounds, and impressions. Texts of Scripture may come to them as from heaven. Their whole souls may be moved, and their confidence in God's favor be undoubting. But in all this there is no religion. The question is, Do they love God's commands, in which his character is fully expressed, and give up to these their habits and passions? Without this, ecstasy is a mockery. One surrender of desire to God's will is worth a thousand transports. We do not judge of the bent of men's minds by their raptures any more than we judge of the natural direction of a tree during a storm. We rather suspect loud profession, for we have observed that deep feeling is generally noiseless and least seeks display.

We would not, by these remarks, be understood as wishing to exclude from religion warmth and even transport. We honor and highly value true religious sensibility. We believe that Christianity is intended to act powerfully on our whole nature, on the heart as well as the understanding and the conscience. We conceive of heaven as a state where the love of God will be exalted into an unbounded fervor and joy; and we desire, in our pilgrimage here, to drink into the spirit of that better world. But we think that religious warmth is only to be valued when it springs naturally from an improved character, when it comes unforced, when it is the recompense of obedience, when it is the warmth of a mind which understands God by being like him, and when, instead of disordering, it exalts the understanding, invigorates conscience, gives a pleasure to common duties, and is seen to exist in connection with cheerfulness, judiciousness, and a reasonable frame of mind. When we observe a fervor called religious in men whose general character expresses little refinement and elevation, and whose piety seems at war with reason, we pay it little respect. We honor religion too much to give its sacred name to a feverish, forced, fluctuating zeal, which has little power over the life.

Another important branch of virtue we believe to be love of Christ. The greatness of the work of Jesus, the spirit with which he executed it, and the sufferings which he bore for our salvation we feel to be strong claims on our gratitude and veneration. We see in nature no beauty to be compared with the loveliness of his character, nor do we find on earth a benefactor to whom we owe an equal debt. We read his history with delight, and learn from it the perfection of our nature. We are particularly touched by his death, which was endured for our redemption, and by that strength of charity which triumphed over his pains. His resurrection is the foundation of our hope of immortality. His intercession gives us boldness to draw nigh to the throne of grace, and we look up to heaven with new desire when we think that, if we follow him here, we shall there see his benignant countenance and enjoy his friendship forever.

I need not express to you our views on the subject of the benevolent virtues. We attach such importance to these that we are sometimes reproached with exalting them above piety. We regard the spirit of love, charity, meekness, forgiveness, liberality, and beneficence as the badge and distinction of Christians, as the brightest image we can bear of God, as the best proof of piety. On this subject I need not and cannot enlarge; but there is one branch of benevolence which I ought not to pass over in silence, because we think that we conceive of it more highly and justly than many of our brethren. I refer to the duty of candor, charitable judgment, especially toward those who differ in religious opinion. We think that in nothing have Christians so widely departed from their religion as in this particular. We read with astonishment and horror the history of the church; and sometimes, when we look back on the fires of persecution, and on the zeal of Christians in building up walls of separation and in giving up one another to perdition, we feel as if we were reading the records of an infernal rather than a heavenly kingdom. An enemy to every religion, if asked to describe a Christian, would, with some show of reason, depict him as an idolater of his own distinguishing opinions, covered with badges of party, shutting his eyes on the virtues and his ears on the arguments of his opponents, arrogating all excellence to his own sect and all saving power to his own creed, sheltering under the name of pious zeal the love of domination, the conceit of infallibility, and the spirit of intolerance, and trampling on men's rights under the pretense of saving their souls.

We can hardly conceive of a plainer obligation on beings of our frail and fallible nature who are instructed in the duty of candid judgment than to abstain from condemning men of apparent conscientiousness and sincerity, who are chargeable with no crime but that of differing from us in the interpretation of the Scriptures, and differing, too, on topics of great and acknowledged obscurity. We are astonished at the hardihood of those who, with Christ's warnings sounding in their ears, take on them the responsibility of making creeds for his church and cast out professors of virtuous lives for imagined errors, for the guilt of thinking for themselves. We know that zeal for truth is the cover for this usurpation of Christ's prerogative; but we think that zeal for truth, as it is called, is very suspicious, except in men whose capacities and advantages, whose patient deliberation and whose improvements in humility, mildness, and candor, give them a right to hope that their views are more just than those of their neighbors. Much of what passes for a zeal for truth we look upon with little respect, for it often appears to thrive most luxuriantly where other virtues shoot up thinly and feebly; and we have no gratitude for those reformers who would force upon us a doctrine which has not sweetened their own tempers, or made them better men than their neighbors.

We are accustomed to think much of the difficulties attending religious inquiries—difficulties springing from the slow development of our minds, from the power of early impressions, from the state of society, from human authority, from the general neglect of the reasoning powers, from the want of just principles of criticism and of important helps in interpreting Scripture, and from various other causes. We find that on no subject have men, and even good men, ingrafted so many strange conceits, wild theories, and fictions of fancy as on religion; and remembering, as we do, that we ourselves are sharers of the common frailty, we dare not assume infallibility in the treatment of our fellow Christians or encourage in common Christians, who have little time for investigation, the habit of denouncing and contemning other denominations, perhaps more enlightened and virtuous than their own. Charity, forbearance, a delight in the virtues of different sects, a backwardness to censure and condemn—these are virtues which, however poorly practiced by us, we admire and recommend; and we would rather join ourselves to the church in which they abound than to any other communion, however elated with the belief of its own orthodoxy, however strict in guarding its creed, however burning with zeal against imagined error.

I have thus given the distinguishing views of those Christians in whose names I have spoken. We have embraced this system, not hastily or lightly, but after much deliberation; and we hold it fast, not merely because we believe it to be true, but because we regard it as purifying truth, as a doctrine according to godliness, as able to "work mightily" and to "bring forth fruit" in them who believe. That we wish to spread it, we have no desire to conceal; but we think that we wish its diffusion because we regard it as more friendly to practical piety and pure morals than the opposite doctrines, because it gives clearer and nobler views of duty and stronger motives to its performance, because it recommends religion at once to the understanding and the heart, because it asserts the lovely and venerable attributes of God, because it tends to restore the benevolent spirit of Jesus to his divided and afflicted church, and because it cuts off every hope of God's favor except that which springs from practical conformity to the life and precepts of Christ. We see nothing in our views to give offense save their purity, and it is their purity which makes us seek and hope their extension through the world.

My friend and brother, you are this day to take upon you important duties; to be clothed with an office which the Son of God did not disdain; to devote yourself to that religion which the most hallowed lips have preached, and the most precious blood sealed. We trust that you will bring to this work a willing mind, a firm purpose, a martyr's spirit, a readiness to toil and suffer for the truth, a devotion of your best powers to the interests of piety and virtue. I have spoken of the doctrines which you will probably preach; but I do not mean that you are to give yourself to controversy. You will remember that good practice is the end of preaching, and will labor to make your people holy livers rather than skillful disputants. Be careful lest the desire of defending what you deem truth, and of repelling reproach and misrepresentation, turn you aside from your great business, which is to fix in men's minds a living conviction of the obligation, sublimity, and happiness of Christian virtue. The best way to vindicate your sentiments is to show, in your preaching and life, their intimate connection with Christian morals, with a high and delicate sense of duty, with candor toward your opposers, with inflexible integrity, and with an habitual reverence for God. If any light can pierce and scatter the clouds of prejudice, it is that of a pure example. My brother, may your life preach more loudly than your lips! Be to this people a pattern of all good works, and may your instructions derive authority from a well-grounded belief in your hearers that you speak from the heart, that you preach from experience, that the truth which you dispense has wrought powerfully in your own heart, that God and Jesus and heaven are not merely words on your lips but most affecting realities to your mind, and springs of hope and consolation and strength in all your trials! Thus laboring, may you reap abundantly and have a testimony of your faithfulness, not only in your own conscience, but in the esteem, love, virtues, and improvements of your people!

To all who hear me I would say, with the Apostle, Prove all things, hold fast that which is good. Do not, brethren, shrink from the duty of searching God's word for yourselves through fear of human censure and denunciation. Do not think that you may innocently follow the opinions which prevail around you, without investigation, on the ground that Christianity is now so purified from errors as to need no laborious research. There is much reason to believe that Christianity is at this moment dishonored by gross and cherished corruptions. If you remember the darkness which hung over the gospel for ages; if you consider the impure union which still subsists in almost every Christian country between the church and state, and which enlists men's selfishness and ambition on the side of established error; if you recollect in what degree the spirit of intolerance has checked free inquiry, not only before but since the Reformation: you will see that Christianity cannot have freed itself from all the human inventions which disfigured it under the Papal tyranny. No. Much stubble is yet to be burned; much rubbish to be removed; many gaudy decorations which a false taste has hung around Christianity must be swept away; and the earth-born fogs which have long shrouded it must be scattered before this divine fabric will rise before us in its native and awful majesty, in its harmonious proportions, in its mild and celestial splendors. This glorious reformation in the church we hope, under God's blessing, from the progress of the human intellect, from the moral progress of society, from the consequent decline of prejudice and bigotry, and, though last not least, from the subversion of human authority in matters of religion, from the fall of those hierarchies and other human institutions by which the minds of individuals are oppressed under the weight of numbers and a Papal dominion is perpetuated in the Protestant church. Our earnest prayer to God is that He will overturn, and overturn, and overturn the strongholds of spiritual usurpation, until HE shall come whose right it is to rule the minds of men; that the conspiracy of ages against the liberty of Christians may be brought to an end; that the servile assent so long yielded to human creeds may give place to honest and devout inquiry into the Scriptures; and that Christianity, thus purified from error, may put forth its almighty energy, and prove itself, by its ennobling influence on the mind, to be indeed "the power of God unto salvation."

THE MORAL ARGUMENT AGAINST CALVINISM

Illustrated in a Review of a Work entitled "A General View of the Doctrines of Christianity, designed more especially for the Edification and Instruction of Families," Boston, 1809.

The work of which we have prefixed the title to this article was published several years ago and has been read by many among us with pleasure and profit. But it is not known as widely as it should be, and we wish to call to it the notice which it merits. It is not an original work, but was compiled chiefly from the writings of the Rev. Robert Fellowes, whose name is probably known to most of our readers. The title we think not altogether happy, because it raises an expectation which the book does not answer. We should expect from it a regular statement of the great truths of our religion; but we find, what at present is perhaps as useful, a vindication of Christianity from the gross errors which Calvinism has labored to identify with this divine system. This may easily be supposed from the table of contents. The book professes to treat of the following subjects: the nature of religion, and the mistakes that occur on that subject; the free agency and accountableness of man; the fall of Adam and original sin; the doctrine of faith in general, and of religious faith in particular; the doctrine of works; the doctrine of regeneration; the doctrine of repentance; the doctrine of grace; the doctrine of election and reprobation; the doctrine of perseverance; the visiting of the iniquities of the fathers upon the children; and the sin against the Holy Ghost. By those who are acquainted with the five thorny points of Calvinism, the design of this compilation will be sufficiently understood from the enumeration of topics now given; and few designs are more praiseworthy than to free Christianity from the reproach brought upon it by that system.[1]

The work under review is professedly popular in its style and mode of discussion. It has little refined and elaborate reasoning, but appeals to the great moral principles of human nature and to the general strain of the Scriptures. It expresses strongly and without circumlocution the abhorrence with which every mind, uncorrupted by false theology, must look on Calvinism; and although some of its delineations may be overcharged, yet they are substantially correct, and their strength is their excellence. The truth is that nothing is so necessary on this subject as to awaken moral feeling in men's breasts. Calvinism owes its perpetuity to the influence of fear in palsying the moral nature. Men's minds and consciences are subdued by terror so that they dare not confess, even to themselves, the shrinking which they feel from the unworthy views which this system gives of God; and, by thus smothering their just abhorrence, they gradually extinguish it, and even come to vindicate in God what would disgrace his creatures. A voice of power and solemn warning is needed to rouse them from this lethargy, to give them a new and a juster dread—the dread of incurring God's displeasure by making him odious and exposing religion to insult and aversion. In the present article we intend to treat this subject with great freedom. But we beg

---

[1] [The principal doctrines of Calvinism were frequently summarized in five points.

(a) Divine Providence: Nature and all created things are sustained and dependent at every moment on the sovereign will of God.

(b) Human Depravity: Man, through his inheritance from Adam and because of his own nature, is completely sinful and deserving of damnation.

(c) Efficacious Grace: Man can be saved only by grace, which is the free gift of God.

(d) Divine Election: God, being completely sovereign in his rule, is under no obligation to save anyone. Being both omniscient and omnipotent He knows from the beginning those who are predestined to be damned and those "elected" for salvation.

(e) Perseverance of the Saints: Those chosen by God, having the power to do his will, manifest their grace in holy perseverance to the end.]

that it may be understood that by Calvinism we intend only the peculiarities or distinguishing features of that system. We would also have it remembered that these peculiarities form a small part of the religious faith of a Calvinist. He joins with them the general, fundamental, and most important truths of Christianity, by which they are always neutralized in a greater or less degree, and in some cases nullified. Accordingly, it has been our happiness to see in the numerous body by which they are professed some of the brightest examples of Christian virtue. Our hostility to the doctrine does not extend to its advocates. In bearing our strongest testimony against error we do not the less honor the moral and religious worth with which it is often connected.

The book under review will probably be objected to by theologians because it takes no notice of a distinction, invented by Calvinistic metaphysicians, for rescuing their doctrines from the charge of aspersing God's equity and goodness. We refer to the distinction between *natural* and *moral inability*—a subtilty which may be thought to deserve some attention because it makes such a show in some of the principal books of this sect.[2] But, with due deference to its defenders, it seems to us groundless and idle—a distinction without a difference. An inability to do our duty which is *born* with us is to all intents, and according to the established meaning of the word, *natural*. Call it moral or what you please, it is still a part of the nature which our Creator gave us, and to suppose that He punishes us for it, because it is an inability

---

[2] [Jonathan Edwards made this distinction famous in his treatise on Free Will (1754). Natural inability, Edwards argued, depends upon physical causes; in this sense we may say that the blind man is physically unable to see. Moral inability depends on moral causes such as "habits and dispositions of the heart, and moral motives and inducements." Although the sinner has the natural (physical) capacity to perform virtue, he is morally unable to do so. Edwards insisted that moral inability is as absolute as natural inability. This distinction helped him to make a rational defense of the doctrines of total depravity and predestination without giving up his notion that the sinner is a free agent.]

seated in the will, is just as absurd as to suppose him to punish us for a weakness of sight or of a limb. Common people cannot understand this distinction, cannot split this hair, and it is no small objection to Calvinism that, according to its ablest defenders, it can only be reconciled to God's perfections by a metaphysical subtilty which the mass of people cannot comprehend.

If we were to speak as critics of the style of this book, we should say that, while generally clear, and sometimes striking, it has the faults of the style which was very current not many years ago in this country, and which, we rejoice to say, is giving place to a better. The style to which we refer, and which threatened to supplant good writing in this country, intended to be elegant but fell into jejuneness and insipidity. It delighted in words and arrangements of words which were little soiled by common use, and mistook a spruce neatness for grace. We had a Procrustes' bed for sentences, and there seemed to be a settled war between the style of writing and the free style of conversation. Times, we think, have changed. Men have learned more to write as they speak, and are ashamed to dress up familiar thoughts as if they were just arrived from a far country and could not appear in public without a foreign and studied attire. They have learned that common words are common precisely because most fitted to express real feeling and strong conception, and that the circuitous, measured phraseology, which was called elegance, was but the parade of weakness. They have learned that words are the signs of thought, and worthless counterfeits without it, and that style is good when, instead of being anxiously cast into a mold, it seems a free and natural expression of thought, and gives to us with power the workings of the author's mind.

We have been led to make these remarks on the style which in a degree marks the book before us from a persuasion that this mode of writing has been particularly injurious to religion, and to rational religion. It has crept into sermons perhaps more than into any other compositions, and has imbued them with that soporific quality which they have sometimes been found to possess in an eminent degree. How many hearers have been soothed by a smooth, watery flow of words, a regular chime of sentences, and elegantly rocked into repose! We are aware that preachers, above all writers, are excusable for this style, because it is the easiest; and, having too much work to do, they must do it, of course, in the readiest way. But we mourn the necessity, and mourn still more the effect. It gives us great pleasure to say that in this particular we think we perceive an improvement taking place in this region. Preaching is becoming more direct, aims more at impression, and seeks the nearest way to men's hearts and consciences. We often hear from the pulpit strong thought in plain and strong language. It is hoped, from the state of society, that we shall not fly from one extreme to another and degenerate into coarseness; but perhaps even this is a less evil than tameness and insipidity.

To return: the principal argument against Calvinism, in the "General View of Christian Doctrines," is the *moral argument,* or that which is drawn from the inconsistency of the system with the divine perfections. It is plain that a doctrine which contradicts our best ideas of goodness and justice cannot come from the just and good God or be a true representation of his character. This moral argument has always been powerful to the pulling down of the strongholds of Calvinism. Even in the dark period when this system was shaped and finished at Geneva, its advocates often writhed under the weight of it; and we cannot but deem it a mark of the progress of society that Calvinists are more and more troubled with the palpable repugnance of their doctrines to God's nature, and accordingly labor to soften and explain them until in many cases the name only is retained. If the stern reformer of Geneva could lift up his head and hear the mitigated tone in which some of his professed followers dispense his fearful doctrines, we fear that he could not lie down in peace until he had poured out his displeasure on their cowardice and degeneracy. He would tell them, with a frown, that *moderate*

Calvinism was a solecism, a contradiction in terms, and would bid them in scorn to join their real friend, Arminius.[3] Such is the power of public opinion and of an improved state of society on creeds, that naked, undisguised Calvinism is not very fond of showing itself, and many of consequence know imperfectly what it means. What, then, is the system against which the "View of Christian Doctrines" is directed?

Calvinism teaches that, in consequence of Adam's sin in eating the forbidden fruit, God brings into life all his posterity with a nature wholly corrupt, so that they are utterly indisposed, disabled, and made opposite to all that is spiritually good and wholly inclined to all evil, and that continually. It teaches that all mankind, having fallen in Adam, are under God's wrath and curse and so made liable to all miseries in this life, to death itself, and to the pains of hell forever. It teaches that from this ruined race God, out of his mere good pleasure, has elected a certain number to be saved by Christ, not induced to this choice by any foresight of their faith or good works but wholly by his free grace and love; and that, having thus predestinated them to eternal life, He renews and sanctifies them by his almighty and special agency, and brings them into a state of grace from which they cannot fall and perish. It teaches that the rest of mankind He is pleased to pass over, and to ordain them to dishonor and wrath for their sins, to the honor of his justice and power; in other words, He leaves the rest to the corruption in which they were born, withholds the grace which is necessary to their recovery, and condemns them to "most grievous torments in soul and body without intermission in hell-fire for ever." Such is Calvinism, as gathered from the most authentic records of the doctrine. Whoever will consult the famous Assembly's Catechisms and Confession will see the peculiarities of the system in all their length and breadth of deformity.[4] A man of plain sense, whose

3 [Jacobus Arminius (1560-1609), Dutch theologian who revolted against the Calvinistic doctrine of predestination.]

4 [The Westminster Assembly of Divines was a famous religious assembly held in the middle of the seventeenth century to provide a general creed

spirit has not been broken to this creed by education or terror, will think that it is not necessary for us to travel to heathen countries to learn how mournfully the human mind may misrepresent the Deity.

The moral argument against Calvinism, of which we have spoken, must seem irresistible to common and unperverted minds after attending to the brief statement now given. It will be asked with astonishment, How is it possible that men can hold these doctrines and yet maintain God's goodness and equity? What principles can be more contradictory? To remove the objection to Calvinism which is drawn from its repugnance to the divine perfections, recourse has been had, as before observed, to the distinction between natural and moral inability, and to other like subtilities. But a more common reply, we conceive, has been drawn from the weakness and imperfection of the human mind, and from its incapacity of comprehending God. Calvinists will tell us that because a doctrine opposes our convictions of rectitude it is not necessarily false; that apparent are not always real inconsistencies; that God is an infinite and incomprehensible Being, and not to be tried by *our* ideas of fitness and morality; that we bring their system to an incompetent tribunal when we submit it to the decision of human reason and conscience; that we are weak judges of what is right and wrong, good and evil, in the Deity; that the happiness of the universe may require an administration of human affairs which is very offensive to limited understandings; that we must follow revelation, not reason or moral feeling, and must consider doctrines which shock us in revelation as awful mysteries, which are dark through our ignorance and which time will enlighten. How little, it is added, can man explain or understand God's ways! How inconsistent the miseries of life appear with goodness in the Creator! How prone, too, have men always been to confound

---

and form of worship for England. Its Confession of Faith (ratified by Parliament in November 1646) and the Shorter Catechism and the Longer Catechism (ratified by Parliament in July 1648) became the standard set of doctrinal articles for Scottish and English Presbyterians.]

good and evil, to call the just unjust! How presumptuous is it in such a being to sit in judgment upon God, and to question the rectitude of the divine administration, because it shocks *his* sense of rectitude! Such we conceive to be a fair statement of the manner in which the Calvinist frequently meets the objection that his system is at war with God's attributes; such the reasoning by which the voice of conscience and nature is stifled and men are reconciled to doctrines which, if tried by the established principles of morality, would be rejected with horror. On this reasoning we purpose to offer some remarks; and we shall avail ourselves of the opportunity to give our views of *the confidence which is due to our rational and moral faculties in religion.*

That God is infinite, and that man often errs, we affirm as strongly as our Calvinistic brethren. We desire to think humbly of ourselves and reverently of our Creator. In the strong language of Scripture, "We now see through a glass darkly." "We cannot by searching find out God unto perfection. Clouds and darkness are round about him. His judgments are a great deep." God is great and good beyond utterance or thought. We have no disposition to idolize our own powers, or to penetrate the secret counsels of the Deity. But, on the other hand, we think it ungrateful to disparage the powers which our Creator has given us, or to question the certainty or importance of the knowledge which He has seen fit to place within our reach. There is an affected humility, we think, as dangerous as pride. We may rate our faculties too meanly as well as too boastingly. The worst error in religion, after all, is that of the skeptic, who records triumphantly the weaknesses and wanderings of the human intellect and maintains that no trust is due to the decisions of this erring reason. We by no means conceive that man's greatest danger springs from pride of understanding, though we think as badly of this vice as other Christians. The history of the church proves that men may trust their faculties too little as well as too much, and that the timidity which shrinks from investigation has injured the mind, and betrayed the interests of Christianity, as much as an irreverent boldness of thought.

It is an important truth, which we apprehend has not been sufficiently developed, that the ultimate reliance of a human being is and must be on his own mind. To confide in God, we must first confide in the faculties by which He is apprehended and by which the proofs of his existence are weighed. A trust in our ability to distinguish between truth and falsehood is implied in every act of belief, for to question this ability would of necessity unsettle all belief. We cannot take a step in reasoning or action without a secret reliance on our own minds. Religion in particular implies that we have understandings endowed and qualified for the highest employments of intellect. In affirming the existence and perfections of God, we suppose and affirm the existence in ourselves of faculties which correspond to these sublime objects and which are fitted to discern them. Religion is a conviction and an act of the human soul, so that in denying confidence to the one, we subvert the truth and claims of the other. Nothing is gained to piety by degrading human nature, for in the competency of this nature to know and judge of God all piety has its foundation. Our proneness to err instructs us, indeed, to use our powers with great caution, but not to contemn and neglect them. The occasional abuse of our faculties, be it ever so enormous, does not prove them unfit for their highest end, which is to form clear and consistent views of God. Because our eyes sometimes fail or deceive us, would a wise man pluck them out or cover them with a bandage and choose to walk and work in the dark? Or, because they cannot distinguish distant objects, can they discern nothing clearly in their proper sphere, and is sight to be pronounced a fallacious guide? Men who, to support a creed, would shake our trust in the calm, deliberate, and distinct decisions of our rational and moral powers endanger religion more than its open foes, and forge the deadliest weapon for the infidel.

It is true that God is an infinite Being, and also true that his powers and perfections, his purposes and operations, his ends and means, being unlimited, are *incomprehensible*. In other words, they cannot be *wholly taken in* or *embraced* by the human mind. In the strong and figurative language of Scripture, we "know nothing" of God's ways; that is, we know *very few* of them. But this is just as true of the most advanced archangel as of man. In comparison with the vastness of God's system, the range of the highest created intellect is narrow; and in this particular man's lot does not differ from that of his elder brethren in heaven. We are both confined in our observation and experience to a little spot in the creation. But are an angel's faculties worthy of no trust, or is his knowledge uncertain, because he learns and reasons from a small part of God's works? Or are his judgments respecting the Creator to be charged with presumption because his views do not spread through the whole extent of the universe? We grant that our understandings cannot stretch beyond a very narrow sphere. But still the lessons which we learn within this sphere are just as sure as if it were indefinitely enlarged. Because much is unexplored, we are not to suspect what we have actually discovered. Knowledge is not the less real because confined. The man who has never set foot beyond his native village knows its scenery and inhabitants as undoubtingly as if he had traveled to the poles. We indeed see very little; but that little is as true as if everything else were seen; and our future discoveries must agree with and support it. Should the whole order and purposes of the universe be opened to us, it is certain that nothing would be disclosed which would in any degree shake our persuasion that the earth is inhabited by rational and moral beings who are authorized to expect from their Creator the most benevolent and equitable government. No extent of observation can unsettle those primary and fundamental principles of moral truth which we derive from our highest faculties operating in the relations in which God has fixed us. In every region and period of the universe it will be as true as it is now on the earth that knowledge and power are the measures of responsibility, and that natural incapacity absolves from guilt. These and other moral verities, which are among our clearest perceptions, would, if possible, be strengthened in proportion as our powers should be enlarged; because harmony and consistency are the characters of God's administration, and all our researches into the universe only serve to manifest its unity and to show a wider operation of the laws which we witness and experience on earth.

We grant that God is *incomprehensible,* in the sense already given. But He is not therefore *unintelligible;* and this distinction we conceive to be important. We do not pretend to know the *whole* nature and properties of God, but still we can form some *clear ideas* of him, and can reason from these ideas as justly as from any other. The truth is that we cannot be said to comprehend any being whatever, not the simplest plant or animal. All have hidden properties. Our knowledge of all is limited. But have we therefore no distinct ideas of the objects around us, and is all our reasoning about them unworthy of trust? Because God is infinite, his name is not therefore a mere sound. It is a representative of some distinct conceptions of our Creator; and these conceptions are as sure and important and as proper materials for the reasoning faculty as they would be if our views were indefinitely enlarged. We cannot indeed trace God's goodness and rectitude through the whole field of his operations; but we know the essential nature of these attributes, and therefore can often judge what accords with and opposes them. God's goodness, because infinite, does not cease to be goodness or essentially differ from the same attribute in man; nor does justice change its nature, so that it cannot be understood, because it is seated in an unbounded mind. There have, indeed, been philosophers, "falsely so called," who have argued from the unlimited nature of God that we cannot ascribe to him justice and other moral attributes in any proper or definite sense of those words; and the inference is plain that all religion or worship, wanting an intelligible object, must be a misplaced, wasted offering. This doctrine from the infidel we reject with abhorrence; but something, not very different, too often reaches us from the mistaken Christian who, to save his creed, shrouds the Creator in utter darkness. In opposition to both, we maintain that God's attributes are intelligible, and that we can conceive as truly of his goodness and justice as of these qualities in men. In fact, these qualities are essentially the same in God and man, though differing in degree, in purity, and in extent of operation. We know not and we cannot conceive of any other justice or goodness than we learn from our own nature; and if God have not these, He is altogether unknown to us as a moral being; He offers nothing for esteem and love to rest upon; the objection of the infidel is just, that worship is wasted: "We worship we know not what."

It is asked, On what authority do we ascribe to God goodness and rectitude in the sense in which these attributes belong to men, or how can we judge of the nature of attributes in the mind of the Creator? We answer by asking, How is it that we become acquainted with the mind of a fellow creature? The last is as invisible, as removed from *immediate* inspection, as the first. Still we do not hesitate to speak of the justice and goodness of a neighbor; and how do we gain our knowledge? We answer, By witnessing the effects, operations, and expressions of these attributes. It is a law of our nature to argue from the effect to the cause, from the action to the agent, from the ends proposed and from the means of pursuing them, to the character and disposition of the being in whom we observe them. By these processes we learn the invisible mind and character of man; and by the same we ascend to the mind of God, whose works, effects, operations, and ends are as expressive and significant of justice and goodness as the best and most decisive actions of men. If this reasoning be sound (and all religion rests upon it), then God's justice and goodness are intelligible attributes, agreeing essentially with the same qualities in ourselves. Their operation, indeed, is infinitely wider, and they are employed in accomplishing not only immediate but remote and unknown ends. Of consequence, we must expect that many parts of the divine administration will be *obscure*, that is, will not produce *immediate* good and an *immediate* distinction between virtue and vice. But still the unbounded operation of these attributes does not change their nature. They are still the same as if they acted in the narrowest sphere. We can still determine in many cases what does not accord with them. We are particularly sure that those essential principles of justice which enter into and even form our conception of this attribute must pervade every province and every period of the administration of a just being, and that to suppose the Creator in any instance to forsake them is to charge him directly with unrighteousness, however loudly the lips may compliment his equity.

"But is it not presumptuous in man," it is continually said, "to sit in judgment on God?" We answer that to "sit in judgment on God" is an ambiguous and offensive phrase, conveying to common minds the ideas of irreverence, boldness, familiarity. The question would be better stated thus: Is it not presumptuous in man to judge concerning God, and concerning what agrees or disagrees with his attributes? We answer confidently, No; for in many cases we are competent and even bound to judge. And we plead first in our defense the Scriptures. How continually does God in his word appeal to the understanding and moral judgment of man! "O inhabitants of Jerusalem and men of Judah, judge, I pray you, between me and my vineyard. What could have been done more to my vineyard, that I have not done in it?" We observe, in the next place, that all religion supposes and is built on judgments passed by us on God and on his operations. Is it not, for example, our duty and a leading part of piety to *praise* God? And what is praising a being but to adjudge and ascribe to him just and generous deeds and motives? And of what value is praise except from those who are capable of distinguishing between actions which exalt and actions which degrade the character? Is it presumptuous to call God *excellent?* And what is this but to refer his character to a standard of excellence, to try it by the established principles of rectitude, and to pronounce its conformity to them: that is, to judge of God and his operations?

We are presumptuous, we are told, in judging of our Creator. But He himself has made this our duty in giving us a moral faculty; and to decline it is to violate the primary law of our nature. Conscience, the sense of right, the power of perceiving moral distinctions, the power of discerning between justice and injustice, excellence and baseness, is the highest faculty given us by God, the whole foundation of our responsibility, and our sole capacity for religion. Now, we are forbidden by this faculty to love a being who wants, or who fails to discover, moral excellence. God, in giving us conscience, has implanted a principle within us which forbids us to prostrate ourselves before mere power, or to offer praise where we do not discover worth—a principle which challenges our supreme homage for supreme goodness, and which absolves us from guilt, when we abhor a severe and unjust administration. Our Creator has consequently waived his own claims on our veneration and obedience any farther than He discovers himself to us in characters of benevolence, equity, and righteousness. He rests his authority on the perfect coincidence of his will and government with those great and fundamental principles of morality written on our souls. He desires no worship but that which springs from the exercise of our moral faculties upon his character, from our discernment and persuasion of his rectitude and goodness. He asks, he accepts, no love or admiration but from those who can understand the nature and the proofs of moral excellence.

There are two or three striking facts which show that there is no presumption in judging of God, and of what agrees or disagrees with his attributes. The first fact is that the most intelligent and devout men have often employed themselves in proving the existence and perfections of God, and have been honored for this service to the cause of religion. Now we ask, What is meant by the *proofs* of a divine perfection? They are certain acts, operations, and methods of government which are proper and natural effects, signs, and expressions of this perfection, and from which, according to the established principles of reasoning, it may be inferred. To prove the divine attributes is to collect and arrange those works and ways of the Creator which accord with these attributes, correspond to them, flow from them, and express them. Of consequence, to prove them requires and implies *the power of judging of what agrees with them,* of discerning their proper marks and expressions. All our treatises on natural theology rest on this power. Every argument in support of a divine perfection is an exercise of it. To deny it is to overthrow all religion.

Now, if such are the proofs of God's goodness and justice, and if we are capable of discerning them, then we are not necessarily presumptuous when we say of particular measures ascribed to him that they are inconsistent with his attributes and cannot belong to him. There is plainly no more presumption in affirming of certain principles of administration that they oppose God's equity and would prove him unrighteous than to affirm of others that they prove him upright and good. There are signs and evidences of injustice as unequivocal as those of justice; and our faculties are as adequate to the perception of the last as of the first. If they must not be trusted in deciding what would prove God unjust, they are unworthy of confidence when they gather evidences of his rectitude; and, of course, the whole structure of religion must fall.

It is no slight objection to the mode of reasoning adopted by the Calvinist that it renders the proof of the divine attributes impossible. When we object to his representations of the divine government that they shock our clearest ideas of goodness and justice, he replies that still they may be true, because we know very little of God, and what seems unjust to man may be in the Creator the perfection of rectitude. Now, this weapon has a double edge. If the strongest marks and expressions of injustice do not prove God unjust, then the strongest marks of the opposite character do not prove him righteous. If the first do not deserve confidence because of our narrow views of God, neither do the last. If, when more shall be known, the first may be found consistent with perfect rectitude, so, when more shall be known, the last may be found consistent with infinite malignity and oppression. This reasoning of our opponents casts us on an ocean of awful uncertainty. Admit it, and we have no proofs of God's goodness and equity to rely upon. What we call proofs may be mere appearances, which a wider knowledge of God may reverse. The future may show us that the very laws and works of the Creator from which we now infer his kindness are consistent with the most determined purpose to spread infinite misery and guilt, and were intended, by raising hope, to add the agony of disappointment to our other woes. Why may not these anticipations, horrible as they are, be verified by the unfolding of God's system if our reasonings about his attributes are rendered so very uncertain, as Calvinism teaches, by the infinity of his nature?

We have mentioned one fact to show that it is not presumptuous to judge of God and of what accords with and opposes his attributes, namely, the fact that his attributes are thought susceptible of proof. Another fact, very decisive on this point, is that Christians of all classes have concurred in resting the truth of Christianity in a great degree on its *internal* evidence, that is, on its accordance with the perfections of God. How common is it to hear from religious teachers that Christianity is worthy of a good and righteous being, that it bears the marks of a divine original! Volumes have been written on its internal proofs, on the coincidence of its purposes and spirit with our highest conceptions of God. How common, too, is it to say of other religions that they are at war with the divine nature, with God's rectitude and goodness, and that we want no other proofs of their falsehood! And what does all this reasoning imply? Clearly this, that we are capable of determining, in many cases, what is worthy and what is unworthy of God, what accords with and what opposes his moral attributes. Deny us this capacity and it would be no presumption against a professed revelation that it ascribed to the Supreme Being the most detestable practices. It might still be said in support of such a system that it is arrogant in man to determine what kind of revelation suits the character of the Creator. Christianity then leans, at least in part, and

THE MORAL ARGUMENT AGAINST CALVINISM   55

some think chiefly, on internal evidence or on its agreeableness to God's moral attributes; and is it probable that this religion, having this foundation, contains representations of God's government which shock our ideas of rectitude, and that it silences our objections by telling us that we are no judges of what suits or opposes his infinite nature?

We will name one more fact to show that it is not presumptuous to form these judgments of the Creator. All Christians are accustomed to reason from God's attributes, and to use them as tests of doctrines. In their controversies with one another they spare no pains to show that their particular views accord best with the divine perfections, and every sect labors to throw on its adversaries the odium of maintaining what is unworthy of God. Theological writings are filled with such arguments; and yet *we,* it seems, are guilty of awful presumption when we deny of God principles of administration against which every pure and good sentiment in our breasts rises in abhorrence.

We shall conclude this discussion with an important inquiry. If God's justice and goodness are consistent with those operations and modes of government which Calvinism ascribes to him, of what use is our belief in these perfections? What expectations can we found upon them? If it consist with divine rectitude to consign to everlasting misery beings who have come guilty and impotent from his hand, we beg to know what interest we have in this rectitude, what pledge of good it contains, or what evil can be imagined which may not be its natural result? If justice and goodness, when stretched to infinity, take such strange forms and appear in such unexpected and apparently inconsistent operations, how are we sure that they will not give up the best men to ruin, and leave the universe to the powers of darkness? Such results, indeed, seem incompatible with these attributes, but not more so than the acts attributed to God by Calvinism. Is it said that the divine faithfulness is pledged in the Scriptures to a happier issue of things? But why should not divine faithfulness transcend our poor understandings as much as divine goodness and justice, and why may not God, consistently with this attribute, crush every hope which his word has raised? Thus all the divine perfections are lost to us as grounds of encouragement and consolation if we maintain that their infinity places them beyond our judgment, and that we must expect from them measures and operations entirely opposed to what seems to us most accordant with their nature.

We have thus endeavored to show that the testimony of our rational and moral faculties against Calvinism is worthy of trust. We know that this reasoning will be met by the question, What, then, becomes of Christianity? For this religion plainly teaches the doctrines you have condemned. Our answer is ready. Christianity contains no such doctrines. Christianity, reason, and conscience are perfectly harmonious on the subject under discussion. Our religion, fairly construed, gives no countenance to that system which has arrogated to itself the distinction of Evangelical. We cannot, however, enter this field at present. We will only say that the general spirit of Christianity affords a very strong presumption that its records teach no such doctrines as we have opposed. This spirit is love, charity, benevolence. Christianity, we all agree, is designed to manifest God as perfect benevolence, and to bring men to love and imitate him. Now, is it probable that a religion, having this object, gives views of the Supreme Being from which our moral convictions and benevolent sentiments shrink with horror, and which, if made our pattern, would convert us into monsters? It is plain that, were a human parent to form himself on the Universal Father as described by Calvinism, that is, were he to bring his children into life totally depraved and then to pursue them with endless punishment, we should charge him with a cruelty not surpassed in the annals of the world; or, were a sovereign to incapacitate his subjects in any way whatever for obeying his laws, and then to torture them in dungeons of perpetual woe, we should say that history records no darker crime. And is it probable that a religion which aims to attract and assimilate us to God, considered as love, should hold him up to us in these heart-

withering characters? We may confidently expect to find in
such a system the brightest views of the divine nature; and
the same objections lie against interpretations of its records,
which savor of cruelty and injustice, as lie against the literal
sense of passages which ascribe to God bodily wants and organs. Let the Scriptures be read with a recollection of the
spirit of Christianity and with that modification of particular
texts by this general spirit which a just criticism requires, and
Calvinism would no more enter the mind of the reader than
Popery—we had almost said, than Heathenism.

In the remarks now made it will be seen, we hope, that we
have aimed to expose doctrines, not to condemn their professors. It is true that men are apt to think themselves assailed
when their system only is called to account. But we have no
foe but error. We are less and less disposed to measure the
piety of others by peculiarities of faith. Men's characters are
determined, not by the opinions which they profess, but by
those on which their thoughts habitually fasten, which recur
to them most forcibly, and which color their ordinary views of
God and duty. The creed of habit, imitation, or fear may be
defended stoutly, and yet have little practical influence. The
mind, when compelled by education or other circumstances
to receive irrational doctrines, has yet a power of keeping
them, as it were, on its surface, of excluding them from its
depths, of refusing to incorporate them with its own being;
and, when burdened with a mixed, incongruous system, it
often discovers a sagacity which reminds us of the instinct of
inferior animals in selecting the healthful and nutritious portions and in making them its daily food. Accordingly, the real
faith often corresponds little with that which is professed. It
often happens that, through the progress of the mind in light
and virtue, opinions, once central, are gradually thrown outward, lose their vitality, and cease to be principles of action,
while through habit they are defended as articles of faith.
The words of the creed survive, but its advocates sympathize
with it little more than its foes. These remarks are particularly applicable to the present subject. A large number, per-

haps a majority, of those who surname themselves with the
name of Calvin have little more title to it than ourselves. They
keep the name and drop the principles which it signifies.
They adhere to the system as a whole but shrink from all its
parts and distinguishing points. This silent but real defection
from Calvinism is spreading more and more widely. The grim
features of this system are softening, and its stern spirit yielding to conciliation and charity. We beg our readers to consult
for themselves the two Catechisms and the Confession of the
Westminster Assembly, and to compare these standards of
Calvinism with what now bears its name. They will rejoice,
we doubt not, in the triumphs of truth. With these views,
we have no disposition to disparage the professors of the system which we condemn, although we believe that its influence
is yet so extensive and pernicious as to bind us to oppose it.

Calvinism, we are persuaded, is giving place to better views.
It has passed its meridian, and is sinking to rise no more. It
has to contend with foes more formidable than theologians;
with foes from whom it cannot shield itself in mystery and
metaphysical subtilties—we mean with the progress of the human mind, and with the progress of the spirit of the gospel.
Society is going forward in intelligence and charity, and of
course is leaving the theology of the sixteenth century behind
it. We hail this revolution of opinion as a most auspicious
event to the Christian cause. We hear much at present of efforts to spread the gospel. But Christianity is gaining more by
the removal of degrading errors than it would by armies of
missionaries who should carry with them a corrupted form of
the religion. We think the decline of Calvinism one of the
most encouraging facts in our passing history; for this system,
by outraging conscience and reason, tends to array these high
faculties against revelation. Its errors are peculiarly mournful
because they relate to the character of God. It darkens and
stains his pure nature, spoils his character of its sacredness,
loveliness, glory, and thus quenches the central light of the
universe, makes existence a curse, and the extinction of it a
consummation devoutly to be wished. We now speak of the

peculiarities of this system, and of their natural influence, when not counteracted, as they always are in a greater or less degree, by better views derived from the spirit and plain lessons of Christianity.

We have had so much to do with our subject that we have neglected to make the usual extracts from the book which we proposed to review. We earnestly wish that a work, answering to the title of this, which should give us "a general view of Christian doctrines," might be undertaken by a powerful hand. Next to a good commentary on the Scriptures, it would be the best service which could be rendered to Christian truth.

THE EVIDENCES OF REVEALED RELIGION

Discourse before the University in Cambridge, at the Dudleian Lecture, 14th March, 1821.

John iii. 2: "The same came to Jesus by night, and said unto him, Rabbi, we know that thou art a teacher come from God; for no man can do these miracles that thou doest, except God be with him."

The evidences of revealed religion are the subject of this lecture—a subject of great extent as well as of vast importance. In discussing it, an immense variety of learning has been employed, and all the powers of the intellect been called forth. History, metaphysics, ancient learning, criticism, ethical science, and the science of human nature have been summoned to the controversy and have brought important contributions to the Christian cause. To condense into one discourse what scholars and great men have written on this point is impossible, even if it were desirable; and I have stated the extent of speculation into which our subject has led, not because I propose to give an abstract of others' labors, but because I wish you to understand that the topic is one not easily dispatched, and because I would invite you to follow me in a discussion which will require concentrated and continued attention. A subject more worthy of attention than the claims of that religion which was impressed on our childhood, and which is acknowledged to be the only firm foundation of the hope of immortality, cannot be presented; and our minds must want the ordinary seriousness of human nature if it cannot arrest us.

That Christianity has been opposed is a fact implied in the establishment of this lecture. That it has had adversaries of no mean intellect, you know. I propose in this discourse to make some remarks on what seems to me the great objection to Christianity, on the general principle on which its evidences rest, and on some of its particular evidences.

The great objection to Christianity—the only one which has much influence at the present day—meets us at the very threshold. We cannot, if we would, evade it, for it is founded on a primary and essential attribute of this religion. The objection is oftener felt than expressed, and amounts to this, that miracles are incredible, and that the supernatural character of an alleged fact is proof enough of its falsehood. So strong is this propensity to doubt of departures from the order of nature that there are sincere Christians who incline to rest their religion wholly on its internal evidence and to overlook the outward extraordinary interposition of God by which it was at first established. But the difficulty cannot in this way be evaded; for Christianity is not only confirmed by miracles, but is in itself, in its very essence, a miraculous religion. It is not a system which the human mind might have gathered in the ordinary exercise of its powers from the ordinary course of nature. Its doctrines, especially those which relate to its Founder, claim for it the distinction of being a supernatural provision for the recovery of the human race. So that the objection which I have stated still presses upon us, and, if it be well grounded, it is fatal to Christianity.

It is proper, then, to begin the discussion with inquiring whence the disposition to discredit miracles springs, and how far it is rational. A preliminary remark of some importance is that this disposition is not a necessary part or principle of our mental constitution, like the disposition to trace effects to adequate causes. We are indeed so framed as to expect a continuance of that order of nature which we have uniformly experienced; but not so framed as to revolt at alleged violations of that order and to account them impossible or absurd. On the contrary, men at large discover a strong and incurable propensity to believe in miracles. Almost all histories, until within the two last centuries, reported seriously supernatural facts. Skepticism as to miracles is comparatively a new thing, if we except the Epicurean or atheistical sect among the ancients; and so far from being founded in human nature, it is resisted by an almost infinite preponderance of belief on the other side.

Whence, then, has this skepticism sprung? It may be explained by two principal causes. (1) It is now an acknowledged fact among enlightened men that in past times and in our own a strong disposition has existed, and still exists, to admit miracles without examination. Human credulity is found to have devoured nothing more eagerly than reports of prodigies. Now it is argued that we discover here a principle of human nature, namely, the love of the supernatural and marvelous, which accounts sufficiently for the belief of miracles wherever we find it; and that it is, consequently, unnecessary and unphilosophical to seek for other causes, and especially to admit that most improbable one—the actual existence of miracles. This sweeping conclusion is a specimen of that rash habit of generalizing which rather distinguishes our times, and shows that philosophical reasoning has made fewer advances than we are apt to boast. It is true that there is a principle of credulity as to prodigies in a considerable part of society, a disposition to believe without due scrutiny. But this principle, like every other in our nature, has its limits; acts according to fixed laws; is not omnipotent—cannot make the eyes see and the ears hear and the understanding credit delusions under all imaginable circumstances; but requires the concurrence of various circumstances and of other principles of our nature in order to its operation. For example, the belief of spectral appearances has been very common; but under what circumstances and in what state of mind has it occurred? Do men see ghosts in broad day and amidst cheerful society? Or in solitary places; in graveyards; in twilights or mists, where outward objects are so undefined as easily to take a form from imagination; and in other circumstances favorable to terror and associated with the delusion in question? The principle of credulity is as regular in its operation as any other principle of the mind; and is so dependent on circumstances and so restrained and checked by other parts of human nature, that sometimes the most obstinate incredulity is found in that very class of people whose easy belief on other occasions moves our contempt. It is well known, for example, that the efficacy of the vaccine inoculation has been encountered with much more unyielding skepticism among the vulgar than among the improved; and in general it may be affirmed that the credulity of the ignorant operates under the control of their strongest passions and impressions, and that no class of society yield a slower assent to positions which manifestly subvert their old modes of thinking and most settled prejudices. It is, then, very unphilosophical to assume this principle as an explanation of all miracles whatever. I grant that the fact that accounts of supernatural agency so generally prove false is a reason for looking upon them with peculiar distrust. Miracles ought on this account to be sifted more than common facts. But if we find that a belief in a series of supernatural works has occurred under circumstances very different from those under which false prodigies have been received, under circumstances most unfavorable to the operation of credulity, then this belief cannot be resolved into the common causes which have blinded men in regard to supernatural agency. We must look for other causes, and if none can be found but the actual existence of the miracles, then true philosophy binds us to believe them. I close this head with observing that the propensity of men to believe in what is strange and miraculous, though a presumption against particular miracles, is not a presumption against miracles universally, but rather the reverse; for great principles of human nature have generally a foundation in truth, and one explanation of this propensity so common to mankind is obviously this, that in the earlier ages of the human race miraculous interpositions, suited to man's infant state, were not uncommon, and, being the most striking facts of human history, they spread through all future times a belief and expectation of miracles.

I proceed now to the second cause of the skepticism in regard to supernatural agency which has grown up, especially among the more improved, in later times. These later times are distinguished, as you well know, by successful researches into nature; and the discoveries of science have continually added strength to that great principle, that the phenomena of the universe are regulated by general and permanent laws, or that the Author of the universe exerts his power according to an established order. Nature, the more it is explored, is found to be uniform. We observe an unbroken succession of causes and effects. Many phenomena, once denominated irregular and ascribed to supernatural agency, are found to be connected with preceding circumstances as regularly as the most common events. The comet, we learn, observes the same attraction as the sun and planets. When a new phenomenon now occurs, no one thinks it miraculous, but believes that, when better understood, it may be reduced to laws already known, or is an example of a law not yet investigated.

Now this increasing acquaintance with the uniformity of nature begets a distrust of alleged violations of it, and a rational distrust, too; for, while many causes of mistake in regard to alleged miracles may be assigned, there is but one adequate cause of real miracles, that is, the power of God; and the regularity of nature forms a strong presumption against the miraculous exertion of this power, except in extraordinary circumstances and for extraordinary purposes to which the established laws of the creation are not competent. But the observation of the uniformity of nature produces, in multitudes, not merely this rational distrust of alleged violations of it, but a secret feeling as if such violations were impossible. That attention to the powers of nature which is implied in scientific research tends to weaken the practical conviction of a higher power; and the laws of the creation, instead of being regarded as the modes of Divine operation, come insensibly to be considered as fetters on his agency—as too sacred to be suspended even by their Author. This secret feeling, essentially atheistical and at war with all sound philosophy, is the chief foundation of that skepticism which prevails in regard to miraculous agency, and deserves our particular consideration.

To a man whose belief in God is strong and practical, a miracle will appear as possible as any other effect, as the most common event in life; and the argument against miracles, drawn from the uniformity of nature, will weigh with him only as far as this uniformity is a pledge and proof of the Creator's disposition to accomplish his purposes by a fixed order or mode of operation. Now it is freely granted that the Creator's regard or attachment to such an order may be inferred from the steadiness with which He observes it; and a strong presumption lies against any violation of it on slight occasions, or for purposes to which the established laws of nature are adequate. But this is the utmost which the order of nature authorizes us to infer respecting its Author. It forms no presumption against miracles universally, in all imaginable cases, but may even furnish a presumption in their favor.

We are never to forget that God's adherence to the order of the universe is not necessary and mechanical but intelligent and voluntary. He adheres to it, not for its own sake or because it has a sacredness which compels him to respect it, but because it is most suited to accomplish his purposes. It is a means, and not an end; and, like all other means, must give way when the end can best be promoted without it. It is the mark of a weak mind to make an idol of order and method to cling to established forms of business when they clog instead of advancing it. If, then, the great purposes of the universe can best be accomplished by departing from its established laws, these laws will undoubtedly be suspended; and though broken in the letter, they will be observed in their spirit, for the ends for which they were first instituted will be advanced by their violation. Now the question arises, For what purposes were nature and its order appointed? And there is no presumption in saying that the highest of these is the improvement of intelligent beings. Mind (by which we mean both moral and intellectual powers) is God's first end. The great purpose for which an order of nature is fixed is plainly the formation of mind. In a creation without order, where events would follow without any regular succession, it is obvious that mind must be kept in perpetual infancy; for, in such a universe, there could be no reasoning from effects to causes, no induction to establish general truths, no adaptation of means to ends; that is, no science relating to God, or matter, or mind; no action; no virtue. The great purpose of God, then, I repeat it, in establishing the order of nature, is to form and advance the mind; and if the case should occur in which the interests of the mind could best be advanced by departing from this order, or by miraculous agency, then the great purpose of the creation, the great end of its laws and regularity, would demand such departure; and miracles, instead of warring against, would concur with nature.

Now we Christians maintain that such a case has existed. We affirm that, when Jesus Christ came into the world, nature had failed to communicate instructions to men in which, as intelligent beings, they had the deepest concern, and on which the full development of their highest faculties essentially depended; and we affirm that there was no prospect of relief from nature; so that an exigence had occurred in which additional communications, supernatural lights, might rationally be expected from the Father of spirits. Let me state two particulars out of many in which men needed intellectual aids not given by nature. I refer to the doctrine of one God and Father, on which all piety rests; and to the doctrine of immortality, which is the great spring of virtuous effort. Had I time to enlarge on the history of that period, I might show you under what heaps of rubbish and superstition these doctrines were buried. But I should repeat only what you know familiarly. The works of ancient genius, which form your studies, carry on their front the brand of polytheism, and of debasing error on subjects of the first and deepest concern. It is more important to observe that the very uniformity of nature had some tendency to obscure the doctrines which I have named, or at least to impair their practical power, so that a departure from this uniformity was needed to fasten them on men's minds.

That a fixed order of nature, though a proof of the One

God to reflecting and enlarged understandings, has yet a tendency to hide him from men in general, will appear if we consider, first, that as the human mind is constituted, what is regular and of constant occurrence excites it feebly; and benefits flowing to it through fixed, unchanging laws seem to come by a kind of necessity and are apt to be traced up to natural causes alone. Accordingly, religious convictions and feelings, even in the present advanced condition of society, are excited not so much by the ordinary course of God's providence as by sudden, unexpected events which rouse and startle the mind and speak of a Power higher than nature. There is another way in which a fixed order of nature seems unfavorable to just impressions respecting its Author. It discovers to us in the Creator a regard to general good rather than an affection to individuals. The laws of nature, operating as they do with an inflexible steadiness, never varying to meet the cases and wants of individuals, and inflicting much private suffering in their stern administration for the general weal, give the idea of a distant, reserved sovereign much more than of a tender parent; and yet this last view of God is the only effectual security from superstition and idolatry. Nature, then, we fear, would not have brought back the world to its Creator. And as to the doctrine of immortality, the order of the natural world had little tendency to teach this, at least with clearness and energy. The natural world contains no provisions or arrangements for reviving the dead. The sun and the rain, which cover the tomb with verdure, send no vital influences to the moldering body. The researches of science detect no secret processes for restoring the lost powers of life. If man is to live again, he is not to live through any known laws of nature, but by a power higher than nature; and how, then, can we be assured of this truth but by a manifestation of this power, that is, by miraculous agency, confirming a future life?

I have labored in these remarks to show that the uniformity of nature is no presumption against miraculous agency when employed in confirmation of such a religion as Christianity. Nature, on the contrary, furnishes a presumption in its favor.

Nature clearly shows to us a power above itself, so that it proves miracles to be possible. Nature reveals purposes and attributes in its Author with which Christianity remarkably agrees. Nature, too, has deficiencies, which show that it was not intended by its Author to be his whole method of instructing mankind; and in this way it gives great confirmation to Christianity, which meets its wants, supplies its chasms, explains its mysteries, and lightens its heart-oppressing cares and sorrows.

Before quitting the general consideration of miracles, I ought to take some notice of Hume's celebrated argument on this subject; not that it merits the attention which it has received, but because it is specious and has derived weight from the name of its author.[1] The argument is briefly this: "That belief is founded upon and regulated by experience. Now we often experience testimony to be false, but never witness a departure from the order of nature. That men may deceive us when they testify to miracles is therefore more accordant with experience than that nature should be irregular; and hence there is a balance of proof against miracles, a presumption so strong as to outweigh the strongest testimony." The usual replies to this argument I have not time to repeat. Dr. Campbell's work, which is accessible to all, will show you that it rests on an equivocal use of terms, and will furnish you with many fine remarks on testimony and on the conditions or qualities which give it validity.[2] I will only add a few remarks which seem to me worthy of attention.

1. This argument affirms that the credibility of facts or statements is to be decided by their accordance with the established order of nature, and by this standard only. Now, if nature comprehended all existences and all powers, this

<hr>

[1] [David Hume (1711-1776), the most influential of eighteenth century English philosophers, made his case against miracles in Section X of *An Inquiry Concerning Human Understanding* first published in London in 1748. Channing's paraphrase of Hume's argument is substantially correct.]

[2] [George Campbell (1719-1796), Scottish theologian whose *Dissertation on Miracles* (1763) was written to refute Hume.]

position might be admitted. But if there is a Being higher than nature, the origin of all its powers and motions, and whose character falls under our notice and experience as truly as the creation, then there is an additional standard to which facts and statements are to be referred; and works which violate nature's order will still be credible if they agree with the known properties and attributes of its Author; because for such works we can assign an adequate cause and sufficient reasons, and these are the qualities and conditions on which credibility depends.

2. This argument of Hume proves too much, and therefore proves nothing. It proves too much: for if I am to reject the strongest testimony to miracles because testimony has often deceived me while nature's order has never been found to fail, then I ought to reject a miracle even if I should see it with my own eyes and if all my senses should attest it; for all my senses have sometimes given false reports, while nature has never gone astray; and, therefore, be the circumstances ever so decisive or inconsistent with deception, still I must not believe what I see and hear and touch—what my senses, exercised according to the most deliberate judgment, declare to be true. All this the argument requires; and it proves too much; for disbelief in the case supposed is out of our power and is instinctively pronounced absurd; and what is more, it would subvert that very order of nature on which the argument rests; for this order of nature is learned only by the exercise of my senses and judgment, and if these fail me in the most unexceptionable circumstances, then their testimony to nature is of little worth.

Once more, this argument is built on an ignorance of the nature of testimony. Testimony, we are told, cannot prove a miracle. Now the truth is that testimony of itself and immediately proves no facts whatever, not even the most common. Testimony can do nothing more than show us the state of another's mind in regard to a given fact. It can only show us that the testifier has a belief, a conviction, that a certain phenomenon or event has occurred. Here testimony stops; and the reality of the event is to be judged altogether from the nature and degree of this conviction and from the circumstances under which it exists. This conviction is an effect, which must have a cause and needs to be explained; and if no cause can be found but the real occurrence of the event, then this occurrence is admitted as true. Such is the extent of testimony. Now a man who affirms a miraculous phenomenon or event may give us just as decisive proofs, by his character and conduct, of the strength and depth of his conviction as if he were affirming a common occurrence. Testimony, then, does just as much in the case of miracles as of common events; that is, it discloses to us the conviction of another's mind. Now this conviction in the case of miracles requires a cause, an explanation, as much as in every other; and if the circumstances be such that it could not have sprung up and been established but by the reality of the alleged miracle, then that great and fundamental principle of human belief, namely, that every effect must have a cause, compels us to admit the miracle.

It may be observed of Hume and of other philosophical opposers of our religion that they are much more inclined to argue against miracles in general than against the particular miracles on which Christianity rests. And the reason is obvious. Miracles, when considered in a general abstract manner —that is, when divested of all circumstances and supposed to occur as disconnected facts, to stand alone in history, to have no explanations or reasons in preceding events and no influence on those which follow—are indeed open to great objection, as wanton and useless violations of nature's order; and it is accordingly against miracles, considered in this naked, general form, that the arguments of infidelity are chiefly urged. But it is great disingenuity to class under this head the miracles of Christianity. They are palpably different. They do not stand alone in history; but are most intimately incorporated with it. They were demanded by the state of the world which preceded them, and they have left deep traces on all subsequent ages. In fact, the history of the whole civilized world, since their alleged occurrence, has been swayed and colored by them, and is wholly inexplicable without them. Now such miracles are not to be met and disposed of by general reasonings which apply only to insulated, unimportant, uninfluential prodigies.

I have thus considered the objections to miracles in general; and I would close this head with observing that these objections will lose their weight just in proportion as we strengthen our conviction of God's power over nature and of his parental interest in his creatures. The great repugnance to the belief of miraculous agency is founded in a lurking atheism, which ascribes supremacy to nature and which, while it professes to believe in God, questions his tender concern for the improvement of men. To a man who cherishes a sense of God, the great difficulty is, not to account for miracles, but to account for their rare occurrence. One of the mysteries of the universe is this, that its Author retires so continually behind the veil of his works, that the great and good Father does not manifest himself more distinctly to his creatures. There is something like coldness and repulsiveness in instructing us only by fixed, inflexible laws of nature. The intercourse of God with Adam and the patriarchs suits our best conceptions of the relation which He bears to the human race, and ought not to surprise us more than the expression of a human parent's tenderness and concern toward his offspring.

After the remarks now made to remove the objection to revelation in general, I proceed to consider the evidences of the Christian religion in particular; and these are so numerous that should I attempt to compress them into the short space which now remains, I could give but a syllabus—a dry and uninteresting index. It will be more useful to state to you, with some distinctness, the general principle into which all Christian evidences may be resolved and on which the whole religion rests, and then to illustrate it in a few striking particulars.

All the evidences of Christianity may be traced to this great principle—that every effect must have an adequate cause. We claim for our religion a divine original because no ade-

quate cause for it can be found in the powers or passions of
human nature, or in the circumstances under which it appeared; because it can only be accounted for by the interposition of that Being to whom its first preachers universally ascribed it, and with whose nature it perfectly agrees.

Christianity, by which we mean not merely the doctrines of
the religion but everything relating to it, its rise, its progress,
the character of its Author, the conduct of its propagators—
Christianity, in this broad sense, can only be accounted for
in two ways. It either sprang from the principles of human
nature, under the excitements, motives, impulses of the age
in which it was first preached, or it had its origin in a higher
and supernatural agency. To which of these causes the religion
should be referred is not a question beyond our reach; for,
being partakers of human nature, and knowing more of it
than of any other part of creation, we can judge with sufficient
accuracy of the operation of its principles and of the effects
to which they are competent. It is indeed true that human
powers are not exactly defined, nor can we state precisely the
bounds beyond which they cannot pass; but still, the disproportion between human nature and an effect ascribed to
it may be so vast and palpable as to satisfy us at once that the
effect is inexplicable by human power. I know not precisely
what advances may be made by the intellect of an unassisted
savage, but that a savage in the woods could not compose the
"Principia" of Newton is about as plain as that he could not
create the world. I know not the point at which bodily
strength must stop, but that a man cannot carry Atlas or
Andes on his shoulders is a safe position. The question, therefore, whether the principles of human nature, under the
circumstances in which it was placed at Christ's birth, will explain his religion, is one to which we are competent, and is
the great question on which the whole controversy turns.

Now we maintain that a great variety of facts belonging to
this religion—such as the character of its Founder; its peculiar
principles; the style and character of its records; its progress;
the conduct, circumstances, and sufferings of its first propaga-

tors; the reception of it from the first on the ground of miraculous attestations; the prophecies which it fulfilled and which it contains; its influence on society, and other circumstances connected with it—are utterly inexplicable by human powers and principles, but accord with, and are fully explained by, the power and perfections of God.

These various particulars I cannot attempt to unfold. One or two may be illustrated to show you the mode of applying the principles which I have laid down. I will take first the character of Jesus Christ. How is this to be explained by the principles of human nature? We are immediately struck with this peculiarity in the Author of Christianity, that while all other men are formed in a measure by the spirit of the age, we can discover in Jesus no impression of the period in which he lived. We know with considerable accuracy the state of society, the modes of thinking, the hopes and expectations of the country in which Jesus was born and grew up; and he is as free from them, and as exalted above them, as if he had lived in another world, or with every sense shut on the objects around him. His character has in it nothing local or temporary. It can be explained by nothing around him. His history shows him to us a solitary being, living for purposes which none but himself comprehended, and enjoying not so much as the sympathy of a single mind. His Apostles, his chosen companions, brought to him the spirit of the age; and nothing shows its strength more strikingly than the slowness with which it yielded in these honest men to the instructions of Jesus.

Jesus came to a nation expecting a Messiah; and he claimed this character. But instead of conforming to the opinions which prevailed in regard to the Messiah, he resisted them wholly and without reserve. To a people anticipating a triumphant leader, under whom vengeance as well as ambition was to be glutted by the prostration of their oppressors, he came as a spiritual leader, teaching humility and peace. This undisguised hostility to the dearest hopes and prejudices of his nation, this disdain of the usual compliances by which ambition and imposture conciliate adherents, this deliberate exposure of himself to rejection and hatred cannot easily be explained by the common principles of human nature, and excludes the possibility of selfish aims in the Author of Christianity.

One striking peculiarity in Jesus is the extent, the vastness, of his views. While all around him looked for a Messiah to liberate God's ancient people, while to every other Jew Judea was the exclusive object of pride and hope, Jesus came declaring himself to be the deliverer and light of the world, and in his whole teaching and life you see a consciousness which never forsakes him of a relation to the whole human race. This idea of blessing mankind, of spreading a universal religion, was the most magnificent which had ever entered man's mind. All previous religions had been given to particular nations. No conqueror, legislator, philosopher, in the extravagance of ambition, had ever dreamed of subjecting all nations to a common faith.

This conception of a universal religion intended alike for Jew and Gentile, for all nations and climes, is wholly inexplicable by the circumstances of Jesus. He was a Jew, and the first and deepest and most constant impression on a Jew's mind was that of the superiority conferred on his people and himself by the national religion introduced by Moses. The wall between the Jew and the Gentile seemed to reach to heaven. The abolition of the peculiarity of Moses, the prostration of the temple on Mount Zion, the erection of a new religion in which all men would meet as brethren and which would be the common and equal property of Jew and Gentile, these were of all ideas the last to spring up in Judea, the last for enthusiasm or imposture to originate.

Compare next these views of Christ with his station in life. He was of humble birth and education, with nothing in his lot, with no extensive means, no rank, or wealth, or patronage, to infuse vast thoughts and extravagant plans. The shop of a carpenter, the village of Nazareth, were not spots for ripening a scheme more aspiring and extensive than had ever been formed. It is a principle of human nature that, except in case of insanity, some proportion is observed between the power of an individual and his plans and hopes. The purpose to which Jesus devoted himself was as ill suited to his condition as an attempt to change the seasons or to make the sun rise in the west. That a young man in obscure life, belonging to an oppressed nation, should seriously think of subverting the time-hallowed and deep-rooted religions of the world is a strange fact; but with this purpose we see the mind of Jesus thoroughly imbued; and, sublime as it is, he never falls below it in his language or conduct, but speaks and acts with a consciousness of superiority, with a dignity and authority, becoming this unparalleled destination.

In this connection I cannot but add another striking circumstance in Jesus, and that is the calm confidence with which he always looked forward to the accomplishment of his design. He fully knew the strength of the passions and powers which were arrayed against him, and was perfectly aware that his life was to be shortened by violence; yet not a word escapes him implying a doubt of the ultimate triumphs of his religion. One of the beauties of the Gospels, and one of the proofs of their genuineness, is found in our Saviour's indirect and obscure allusions to his approaching sufferings and to the glory which was to follow—allusions showing us the workings of a mind thoroughly conscious of being appointed to accomplish infinite good through great calamity. This entire and patient relinquishment of immediate success, this ever-present persuasion that he was to perish before his religion would advance, and this calm, unshaken anticipation of distant and unbounded triumphs are remarkable traits, throwing a tender and solemn grandeur over our Lord, and wholly inexplicable by human principles or by the circumstances in which he was placed.

The views hitherto taken of Christ relate to his public character and office. If we pass to what may be called his private character, we shall receive the same impression of inexplicable excellence. The most striking trait in Jesus was, undoubtedly, benevolence; and although this virtue had existed before, yet it had not been manifested in the same form and extent. Christ's benevolence was distinguished first by its expansiveness. At that age an unconfined philanthropy, proposing and toiling to do good without distinction of country or rank, was unknown. Love to man as man, love comprehending the hated Samaritan and the despised publican, was a feature which separated Jesus from the best men of his nation and of the world. Another characteristic of the benevolence of Jesus was its gentleness and tenderness, forming a strong contrast with the hardness and ferocity of the spirit and manners which then prevailed, and with that sternness and inflexibility which the purest philosophy of Greece and Rome inculcated as the perfection of virtue. But its most distinguishing trait was its superiority to injury. Revenge was one of the recognized rights of the age in which he lived; and though a few sages who had seen its inconsistency with man's dignity had condemned it, yet none had inculcated the duty of regarding one's worst enemies with that kindness which God manifests to sinful men, and of returning curses with blessings and prayers. This form of benevolence, the most disinterested and divine form, was, as you well know, manifested by Jesus Christ in infinite strength, amidst injuries and indignities which cannot be surpassed. Now this singular eminence of goodness, this superiority to the degrading influences of the age under which all other men suffered, needs to be explained; and one thing it demonstrates, that Jesus Christ was not an unprincipled deceiver, exposing not only his own life but the lives of confiding friends in an enterprise next to desperate.

I cannot enlarge on other traits of the character of Christ. I will only observe that it had one distinction which more than anything forms a perfect character. It was made up of contrasts; in other words, it was a union of excellences which are not easily reconciled, which seem at first sight incongruous, but which, when blended and duly proportioned, constitute moral harmony and attract with equal power love and veneration. For example, we discover in Jesus Christ an unparalleled dignity of character, a consciousness of greatness never discovered or approached by any other individual in history; and yet this was blended with a condescension, lowliness, and unostentatious simplicity which had never before been thought consistent with greatness. In like manner, he united an utter superiority to the world, to its pleasures and ordinary interests, with suavity of manners and freedom from austerity. He joined strong feeling and self-possession, an indignant sensibility to sin and compassion to the sinner, an intense devotion to his work and calmness under opposition and ill success, a universal philanthropy and a susceptibility of private attachments, the authority which became the Saviour of the world and the tenderness and gratitude of a son. Such was the Author of our religion. And is his character to be explained by imposture or insane enthusiasm? Does it not bear the unambiguous marks of a heavenly origin?

Perhaps it may be said this character never existed. Then the invention of it is to be explained, and the reception which this fiction met with; and these perhaps are as difficult of explanation on natural principles as its real existence. Christ's history bears all the marks of reality; a more frank, simple, unlabored, unostentatious narrative was never penned. Besides, his character, if invented, must have been an invention of singular difficulty, because no models existed on which to frame it. He stands alone in the records of time. The conception of a being proposing such new and exalted ends and governed by higher principles than the progress of society had developed implies singular intellectual power. That several individuals should join in equally vivid conceptions of this character, and should not merely describe in general terms the fictitious being to whom it was attributed but should introduce him into real life, should place him in a great variety of circumstances, in connection with various ranks of men, with friends and foes, and should in all preserve his identity, show the same great and singular mind always acting in harmony with itself: this is a supposition hardly credible, and, when the circumstances of the writers of the New Testament are considered, seems to be as inexplicable on human principles as what I before suggested, the composition of Newton's "Principia" by a savage. The character of Christ, though delineated in an age of great moral darkness, has stood the scrutiny of ages; and, in proportion as men's moral sentiments have been refined, its beauty has been more seen and felt. To suppose it invented is to suppose that its authors, outstripping their age, had attained to a singular delicacy and elevation of moral perception and feeling. But these attainments are not very reconcilable with the character of its authors, supposing it to be a fiction; that is, with the character of habitual liars and impious deceivers.

But we are not only unable to discover powers adequate to this invention. There must have been motives for it; for men do not make great efforts without strong motives; and, in the whole compass of human incitements, we challenge the infidel to suggest any which could have prompted to the work now to be explained.

Once more, it must be recollected that this invention, if it were one, was received as real at a period so near to the time ascribed to Christ's appearance that the means of detecting it were infinite. That men should send out such a forgery, and that it should prevail and triumph, are circumstances not easily reconcilable with the principles of our nature.

The character of Christ, then, was real. Its reality is the only explanation of the mighty revolution produced by his religion. And how can you account for it, but by that cause to which he always referred it—a mission from the Father?

Next to the character of Christ, his religion might be shown to abound in circumstances which contradict and repel the idea of a human origin. For example, its representations of the paternal character of God; its inculcation of a universal charity; the stress which it lays on inward purity; its substitution of a spiritual worship for the forms and ceremonies which everywhere had usurped the name and extinguished the life of religion; its preference of humility and of the mild, unostentatious, passive virtues to the dazzling qualities which had monopolized men's admiration; its consistent and bright discoveries of immortality; its adaptation to the wants of man as a sinner; its adaptation to all the conditions, capacities, and sufferings of human nature; its pure, sublime, yet practicable morality; its high and generous motives; and its fitness to form a character which plainly prepares for a higher life than the present: these are peculiarities of Christianity which will strike us more and more in proportion as we understand distinctly the circumstances of the age and country in which this religion appeared, and for which no adequate human cause has been or can be assigned.

Passing over these topics, each of which might be enlarged into a discourse, I will make but one remark on this religion, which strikes my own mind very forcibly. Since its introduction, human nature has made great progress and society experienced great changes; and in this advanced condition of the world Christianity, instead of losing its application and importance, is found to be more and more congenial and adapted to man's nature and wants. Men have outgrown the other institutions of that period when Christianity appeared—its philosophy, its modes of warfare, its policy, its public and private economy; but Christianity has never shrunk as intellect has opened, but has always kept in advance of men's faculties and unfolded nobler views in proportion as they have ascended. The highest powers and affections which our nature has developed find more than adequate objects in this religion. Christianity is, indeed, peculiarly fitted to the more improved stages of society, to the more delicate sensibilities of refined minds, and especially to that dissatisfaction with the present state which always grows with the growth of our moral powers and affections. As men advance in civilization, they become susceptible of mental sufferings to which ruder ages are strangers; and these Christianity is fitted to assuage. Imagination and intellect become more restless; and Christianity brings them tranquillity by the eternal and magnificent truths, the solemn and unbounded prospects, which it unfolds. This fitness of our religion to more advanced stages of society than that in which it was introduced, to wants of human nature not then developed, seems to me very striking. The religion bears the marks of having come from a Being who perfectly understood the human mind and had power to provide for its progress. This feature of Christianity is of the nature of prophecy. It was an anticipation of future and distant ages; and, when we consider among whom our religion sprang, where but in God can we find an explanation of this peculiarity?

I have now offered a few hints on the character of Christ and on the character of his religion; and before quitting these topics I would observe that they form a strong presumption in favor of the miraculous facts of the Christian history. These miracles were not wrought by a man whose character in other respects was ordinary. They were acts of a being whose mind was as singular as his works, who spoke and acted with more than human authority, whose moral qualities and sublime purposes were in accordance with superhuman powers. Christ's miracles are in unison with his whole character, and bear a proportion to it like that which we observe in the most harmonious productions of nature; and in this way they receive from it great confirmation. And the same presumption in their favor arises from his religion. That a religion carrying in itself such marks of divinity, and so inexplicable on human principles, should receive outward confirmations from Omnipotence is not surprising. The extraordinary character of the religion accords with and seems to demand extraordinary interpositions in its behalf. Its miracles are not solitary, naked, unexplained, disconnected events, but are bound up with a system which is worthy of God, and impressed with God; which occupies a large space, and is operating with great and increasing energy in human affairs.

As yet I have not touched on what seem to many writers the strongest proofs of Christianity—I mean the direct evidences of its miracles, by which we mean the testimony borne to them, including the character, conduct, and condition of the witnesses. These I have not time to unfold; nor is this labor needed, for Paley's inestimable work, which is one of your classical books, has stated these proofs with great clearness and power.[3] I would only observe that they may all be resolved into this single principle, namely, that the Christian miracles were originally believed under such circumstances that this belief can only be explained by their actual occurrence. That Christianity was received at first on the ground of miracles, and that its first preachers and converts proved the depth and strength of their conviction of these facts by attesting them in sufferings and in death, we know from the most ancient records which relate to this religion, both Christian and heathen; and, in fact, this conviction can alone explain their adherence to Christianity. Now, that this conviction could only have sprung from the reality of the miracles we infer from the known circumstances of these witnesses, whose passions, interests, and strongest prejudices were originally hostile to the new religion; whose motives for examining with care the facts on which it rested were as urgent and solemn, and whose means and opportunities of ascertaining their truth were as ample and unfailing, as can be conceived to conspire; so that the supposition of their falsehood cannot be admitted without subverting our trust in human judgment and human testimony under the most favorable circumstances for discovering truth; that is, without introducing universal skepticism.

There is one class of Christian evidences to which I have but slightly referred but which has struck with peculiar force men of reflecting minds. I refer to the marks of truth and reality which are found in the Christian records; to the internal proofs which the books of the New Testament carry with them of having been written by men who lived in the first

---

[3] [William Paley (1743-1805), prominent English churchman and theologian, whose *Natural Theology, or Evidences of the Existence and Attributes of the Deity Collected from the Appearances of Nature* was published in 1802. This book, a classic example of the argument that the orderliness of nature implies the existence of an intelligent creator, was a standard text in most American colleges during the early nineteenth century.]

age of Christianity, who believed and felt its truth, who bore a part in the labors and conflicts which attended its establishment, and who wrote from personal knowledge and deep conviction. A few remarks to illustrate the nature and power of these internal proofs, which are furnished by the books of the New Testament, I will now subjoin.

The New Testament consists of histories and epistles. The historical books, namely, the Gospels and the Acts, are a continued narrative embracing many years and professing to give the history of the rise and progress of the religion. Now it is worthy of observation that these writings completely answer their end; that they completely solve the problem, how this peculiar religion grew up and established itself in the world; that they furnish precise and adequate causes for this stupendous revolution in human affairs. It is also worthy of remark that they relate a series of facts which are not only connected with one another, but are intimately linked with the long series which has followed them, and agree accurately with subsequent history, so as to account for and sustain it. Now, that a collection of fictitious narratives coming from different hands, comprehending many years, and spreading over many countries should not only form a consistent whole when taken by themselves, but should also connect and interweave themselves with real history so naturally and intimately as to furnish no clue for detection, as to exclude the appearance of incongruity and discordance, and as to give an adequate explanation, and the only explanation, of acknowledged events, of the most important revolution in society—this is a supposition from which an intelligent man at once revolts, and which, if admitted, would shake a principal foundation of history.

I have before spoken of the unity and consistency of Christ's character as developed in the Gospels, and of the agreement of the different writers in giving us the singular features of his mind. Now there are the same marks of truth running through the whole of these narratives. For example, the effects produced by Jesus on the various classes of society; the different feelings of admiration, attachment, and envy which he called forth; the various expressions of these feelings; the prejudices, mistakes, and gradual illumination of his disciples—these are all given to us with such marks of truth and reality as could not easily be counterfeited. The whole history is precisely such as might be expected from the actual appearance of such a person as Jesus Christ, in such a state of society as then existed.

The Epistles, if possible, abound in marks of truth and reality even more than the Gospels. They are imbued thoroughly with the spirit of the first age of Christianity. They bear all the marks of having come from men plunged in the conflicts which the new religion excited, alive to its interests, identified with its fortunes. They betray the very state of mind which must have been generated by the peculiar condition of the first propagators of the religion. They are letters written on real business, intended for immediate effects, designed to meet prejudices and passions which such a religion must at first have awakened. They contain not a trace of the circumstances of a later age, or of the feelings, impressions, and modes of thinking by which later times were characterized and from which later writers could not easily have escaped. The letters of Paul have a remarkable agreement with his history. They are precisely such as might be expected from a man of a vehement mind who had been brought up in the schools of Jewish literature, who had been converted by a sudden, overwhelming miracle, who had been entrusted with the preaching of the new religion to the Gentiles, and who was everywhere met by the prejudices and persecuting spirit of his own nation. They are full of obscurities growing out of these points of Paul's history and character and out of the circumstances of the infant church, and which nothing but an intimate acquaintance with that early period can illustrate. This remarkable infusion of the spirit of the first age into the Christian records cannot easily be explained but by the fact that they were written in that age by the real and zealous propagators of Christianity, and that they are records of real convictions and of actual events.

There is another evidence of Christianity still more internal than any on which I have yet dwelt—an evidence to be felt rather than described, but not less real because founded on feeling. I refer to that conviction of the divine original of our religion which springs up and continually gains strength in those who apply it habitually to their tempers and lives, and who imbibe its spirit and hopes. In such men there is a consciousness of the adaptation of Christianity to their noblest faculties—a consciousness of its exalting and consoling influences, of its power to confer the true happiness of human nature, to give that peace which the world cannot give—which assures them that it is not of earthly origin but a ray from the Everlasting Light, a stream from the Fountain of heavenly wisdom and love. This is the evidence which sustains the faith of thousands who never read and cannot understand the learned books of Christian apologists, who want, perhaps, words to explain the ground of their belief, but whose faith is of adamantine firmness, who hold the Gospel with a conviction more intimate and unwavering than mere argument ever produced.

But I must tear myself from a subject which opens upon me continually as I proceed. Imperfect as this discussion is, the conclusion, I trust, is placed beyond doubt, that Christianity is true. And, my hearers, if true, it is the greatest of all truths, deserving and demanding our reverent attention and fervent gratitude. This religion must never be confounded with our common blessings. It is a revelation of pardon which, as sinners, we all need. Still more, it is a revelation of human immortality—a doctrine which, however undervalued amidst the bright anticipations of inexperienced youth, is found to be our strength and consolation, and the only effectual spring of persevering and victorious virtue, when the realities of life have scattered our visionary hopes; when pain, disappointment, and temptation press upon us; when this world's enjoyments are found unable to quench that deep thirst of happiness which burns in every breast; when friends whom we love as our own souls, die; and our own graves open before us. To all who hear me, and especially to my young hearers, I would say, let the truth of this religion be the strongest conviction of your understandings; let its motives and precepts sway with an absolute power your characters and lives.

LIKENESS TO GOD

Discourse at the Ordination of the Rev. F. A. Farley,
Providence, R. I., 1828.

Eph. v. 1: "Be ye therefore followers of God,
as dear children."

To promote true religion is the purpose of the Christian
ministry. For this it was ordained. On the present occasion,
therefore, when a new teacher is to be given to the church, a
discourse on the character of true religion will not be inap-
propriate. I do not mean that I shall attempt, in the limits to
which I am now confined, to set before you all its properties,
signs, and operations; for in so doing I should burden your
memories with divisions and vague generalities as uninteresting as they would be unprofitable. My purpose is to select one
view of the subject which seems to me of primary dignity and
importance; and I select this because it is greatly neglected,
and because I attribute to this neglect much of the inefficacy
and many of the corruptions of religion.

The text calls us to follow or imitate God, to seek accordance with or likeness to him; and to do this not fearfully and
faintly, but with the spirit and hope of beloved children. The
doctrine which I propose to illustrate is derived immediately
from these words, and is incorporated with the whole New
Testament. I affirm, and would maintain, that true religion
consists in proposing, as our great end, a growing likeness to
the Supreme Being. Its noblest influence consists in making
us more and more partakers of the Divinity. For this it is to be
preached. Religious instruction should aim chiefly to turn
men's aspirations and efforts to that perfection of the soul
which constitutes it a bright image of God. Such is the topic
now to be discussed; and I implore Him whose glory I seek to

aid me in unfolding and enforcing it with simplicity and clearness, with a calm and pure zeal, and with unfeigned charity.

I begin with observing, what all indeed will understand, that the likeness to God, of which I propose to speak, belongs to man's higher or spiritual nature. It has its foundation in the original and essential capacities of the mind. In proportion as these are unfolded by right and vigorous exertion, it is extended and brightened. In proportion as these lie dormant, it is obscured. In proportion as they are perverted and overpowered by the appetites and passions, it is blotted out. In truth, moral evil, if unresisted and habitual, may so blight and lay waste these capacities that the image of God in man may seem to be wholly destroyed.

The importance of this assimilation to our Creator is a topic which needs no labored discussion. All men, of whatever name, or sect, or opinion, will meet me on this ground. All, I presume, will allow that no good in the compass of the universe, or within the gift of omnipotence, can be compared to a resemblance of God, or to a participation of his attributes. I fear no contradiction here. Likeness to God is the supreme gift. He can communicate nothing so precious, glorious, blessed as himself. To hold intellectual and moral affinity with the Supreme Being, to partake his spirit, to be his children by derivations of kindred excellence, to bear a growing conformity to the perfection which we adore—this is a felicity which obscures and annihilates all other good.

It is only in proportion to this likeness that we can enjoy either God or the universe. That God can be known and enjoyed only through sympathy or kindred attributes is a doctrine which even Gentile philosophy discerned. That the pure in heart can alone see and commune with the pure Divinity was the sublime instruction of ancient sages as well as of inspired prophets. It is indeed the lesson of daily experience. To understand a great and good being, we must have the seeds of the same excellence. How quickly, by what an instinct, do accordant minds recognize one another! No attraction is so powerful as that which subsists between the truly wise and good; while the brightest excellence is lost on those who have nothing congenial in their own breasts. God becomes a real being to us in proportion as his own nature is unfolded within us. To a man who is growing in the likeness of God, faith begins even here to change into vision. He carries within himself a proof of a Deity which can only be understood by experience. He more than believes, he feels the Divine presence; and gradually rises to an intercourse with his Maker to which it is not irreverent to apply the name of friendship and intimacy. The Apostle John intended to express this truth when he tells us that he in whom a principle of divine charity or benevolence has become a habit and life "dwells in God and God in him."

It is plain, too, that likeness to God is the true and only preparation for the enjoyment of the universe. In proportion as we approach and resemble the mind of God, we are brought into harmony with the creation; for in that proportion we possess the principles from which the universe sprang; we carry within ourselves the perfections of which its beauty, magnificence, order, benevolent adaptations, and boundless purposes are the results and manifestations. God unfolds himself in his works to a kindred mind. It is possible that the brevity of these hints may expose to the charge of mysticism what seems to me the calmest and clearest truth. I think, however, that every reflecting man will feel that likeness to God must be a principle of sympathy or accordance with his creation; for the creation is a birth and shining forth of the Divine Mind, a work through which his spirit breathes. In proportion as we receive this spirit we possess within ourselves the explanation of what we see. We discern more and more of God in everything, from the frail flower to the everlasting stars. Even in evil, that dark cloud which hangs over the creation, we discern rays of light and hope, and gradually come to see, in suffering and temptation, proofs and instruments of the sublimest purposes of wisdom and love.

I have offered these very imperfect views that I may show

the great importance of the doctrine which I am solicitous to enforce. I would teach that likeness to God is a good so unutterably surpassing all other good that whoever admits it as attainable must acknowledge it to be the chief aim of life. I would show that the highest and happiest office of religion is to bring the mind into growing accordance with God; and that by the tendency of religious systems to this end their truth and worth are to be chiefly tried.

I am aware that it may be said that the Scriptures, in speaking of man as made in the image of God, and in calling us to imitate him, use bold and figurative language. It may be said that there is danger from too literal an interpretation; that God is an unapproachable being; that I am not warranted in ascribing to man a like nature to the divine; that we and all things illustrate the Creator by contrast, not by resemblance; that religion manifests itself chiefly in convictions and acknowledgments of utter worthlessness; and that to talk of the greatness and divinity of the human soul is to inflate that pride through which Satan fell, and through which man involves himself in that fallen spirit's ruin.

I answer that, to me, Scripture and reason hold a different language. In Christianity, particularly, I meet perpetual testimonies to the divinity of human nature. This whole religion expresses an infinite concern of God for the human soul, and teaches that He deems no methods too expensive for its recovery and exaltation. Christianity, with one voice, calls me to turn my regards and care to the spirit within me, as of more worth than the whole outward world. It calls us to "be perfect as our Father in heaven is perfect"; and everywhere, in the sublimity of its precepts, it implies and recognizes the sublime capacities of the being to whom they are addressed. It assures us that human virtue is "in the sight of God of great price," and speaks of the return of a human being to virtue as an event which increases the joy of heaven. In the New Testament, Jesus Christ, the Son of God, the brightness of his glory, the express and unsullied image of the Divinity, is seen mingling with men as a friend and brother, offering himself as their example, and promising to his true followers a share in all his splendors and joys. In the New Testament God is said to communicate his own spirit and all his fullness to the human soul. In the New Testament man is exhorted to aspire after "honor, glory, and immortality"; and heaven, a word expressing the nearest approach to God and a divine happiness, is everywhere proposed as the end of his being. In truth, the very essence of Christian faith is that we trust in God's mercy as revealed in Jesus Christ, for a state of celestial purity in which we shall grow forever in the likeness and knowledge and enjoyment of the Infinite Father. Lofty views of the nature of man are bound up and interwoven with the whole Christian system. Say not that these are at war with humility; for who was ever humbler than Jesus, and yet who ever possessed such a consciousness of greatness and divinity? Say not that man's business is to think of his sin and not of his dignity; for great sin implies a great capacity; it is the abuse of a noble nature; and no man can be deeply and rationally contrite but he who feels that in wrongdoing he has resisted a divine voice, and warred against a divine principle in his own soul. I need not, I trust, pursue the argument from revelation. There is an argument from nature and reason which seems to me so convincing, and is at the same time so fitted to explain what I mean by man's possession of a like nature to God, that I shall pass at once to its exposition.

That man has a kindred nature with God, and may bear most important and ennobling relations to him, seems to me to be established by a striking proof. This proof you will understand by considering for a moment how we obtain our ideas of God. Whence come the conceptions which we include under that august name? Whence do we derive our knowledge of the attributes and perfections which constitute the Supreme Being? I answer, we derive them from our own souls. The divine attributes are first developed in ourselves and thence transferred to our Creator. The idea of God, sublime and awful as it is, is the idea of our own spiritual nature, purified and enlarged to infinity. In ourselves are the elements of the

Divinity. God, then, does not sustain a figurative resemblance to man. It is the resemblance of a parent to a child, the likeness of a kindred nature.

We call God a Mind. He has revealed himself as a Spirit. But what do we know of mind but through the unfolding of this principle in our own breasts? That unbounded spiritual energy which we call God is conceived by us only through consciousness, through the knowledge of ourselves. We ascribe thought or intelligence to the Deity as one of his most glorious attributes. And what means this language? These terms we have framed to express operations or faculties of our own souls. The Infinite Light would be forever hidden from us did not kindred rays dawn and brighten within us. God is another name for human intelligence raised above all error and imperfection, and extended to all possible truth.

The same is true of God's goodness. How do we understand this but by the principle of love implanted in the human breast? Whence is it that this divine attribute is so faintly comprehended, but from the feeble development of it in the multitude of men? Who can understand the strength, purity, fullness, and extent of divine philanthropy, but he in whom selfishness has been swallowed up in love?

The same is true of all the moral perfections of the Deity. These are comprehended by us only through our own moral nature. It is conscience within us which, by its approving and condemning voice, interprets to us God's love of virtue and hatred of sin; and without conscience, these glorious conceptions would never have opened on the mind. It is the lawgiver in our own breasts which gives us the idea of divine authority, and binds us to obey it. The soul, by its sense of right or its perception of moral distinctions, is clothed with sovereignty over itself, and through this alone it understands and recognizes the Sovereign of the universe. Men, as by a natural inspiration, have agreed to speak of conscience as the voice of God, as the Divinity within us. This principle, reverently obeyed, makes us more and more partakers of the moral perfection of the Supreme Being, of that very excellence which

constitutes the rightfulness of his scepter and enthrones him
over the universe. Without this inward law we should be as
incapable of receiving a law from heaven as the brute. Without this, the thunders of Sinai might startle the outward ear,
but would have no meaning, no authority, to the mind. I have
expressed here a great truth. Nothing teaches so encourag-
ingly our relation and resemblance to God; for the glory of
the Supreme Being is eminently moral. We blind ourselves
to his chief splendor if we think only or mainly of his power,
and overlook those attributes of rectitude and goodness to
which He subjects his omnipotence, and which are the foundations and very substance of his universal and immutable
law. And are these attributes revealed to us through the
principles and convictions of our own souls? Do we understand through sympathy God's perception of the right, the
good, the holy, the just? Then with what propriety is it said
that in his own image He made man!

I am aware that it may be objected to these views that we
receive our idea of God from the universe, from his works,
and not so exclusively from our own souls. The universe, I
know, is full of God. The heavens and earth declare his glory.
In other words, the effects and signs of power, wisdom, and
goodness are apparent through the whole creation. But apparent to what? Not to the outward eye; not to the acutest
organs of sense; but to a kindred mind, which interprets the
universe by itself. It is only through that energy of thought by
which we adapt various and complicated means to distant
ends, and give harmony and a common bearing to multiplied
exertions, that we understand the creative intelligence which
has established the order, dependencies, and harmony of nature. We see God around us because He dwells within us. It
is by a kindred wisdom that we discern his wisdom in his
works. The brute, with an eye as piercing as ours, looks on
the universe; and the page, which to us is radiant with characters of greatness and goodness, is to him a blank. In truth,
the beauty and glory of God's works are revealed to the mind
by a light beaming from itself. We discern the impress of

God's attributes in the universe by accordance of nature, and enjoy them through sympathy. I hardly need observe that these remarks in relation to the universe apply with equal if not greater force to revelation.

I shall now be met by another objection, which to many may seem strong. It will be said that these various attributes of which I have spoken exist in God in infinite perfection, and that this destroys all affinity between the human and the divine mind. To this I have two replies. In the first place, an attribute by becoming perfect does not part with its essence. Love, wisdom, power, and purity do not change their nature by enlargement. If they did, we should lose the Supreme Being through his very infinity. Our ideas of him would fade away into mere sounds. For example, if wisdom in God, because unbounded, have no affinity with that attribute in man, why apply to him that term? It must signify nothing. Let me ask what we mean when we say that we discern the marks of intelligence in the universe? We mean that we meet there the proofs of a mind like our own. We certainly discern proofs of no other; so that to deny this doctrine would be to deny the evidences of a God, and utterly to subvert the foundations of religious belief. What man can examine the structure of a plant or an animal, and see the adaptation of its parts to each other and to common ends, and not feel that it is the work of an intelligence akin to his own, and that he traces these marks of design by the same spiritual energy in which they had their origin?

But I would offer another answer to this objection, that God's infinity places him beyond the resemblance and approach of man. I affirm, and trust that I do not speak too strongly, that there are traces of infinity in the human mind; and that, in this very respect, it bears a likeness to God. The very conception of infinity is the mark of a nature to which no limit can be prescribed. This thought, indeed, comes to us not so much from abroad as from our own souls. We ascribe this attribute to God because we possess capacities and wants which only an unbounded being can fill, and because we are conscious of a tendency in spiritual faculties to unlimited expansion. We believe in the divine infinity through something congenial with it in our own breasts. I hope I speak clearly, and if not, I would ask those to whom I am obscure to pause before they condemn. To me it seems that the soul, in all its higher actions, in original thought, in the creations of genius, in the soarings of imagination, in its love of beauty and grandeur, in its aspirations after a pure and unknown joy, and especially in disinterestedness, in the spirit of self-sacrifice, and in enlightened devotion, has a character of infinity. There is often a depth in human love which may be strictly called unfathomable. There is sometimes a lofty strength in moral principle which all the power of the outward universe cannot overcome. There seems a might within which can more than balance all might without. There is, too, a piety which swells into a transport too vast for utterance, and into an immeasurable joy. I am speaking, indeed, of what is uncommon, but still of realities. We see, however, the tendency of the soul to the infinite in more familiar and ordinary forms. Take, for example, the delight which we find in the vast scenes of nature, in prospects which spread around us without limits, in the immensity of the heavens and the ocean, and especially in the rush and roar of mighty winds, waves, and torrents when, amidst our deep awe, a power within seems to respond to the omnipotence around us. The same principle is seen in the delight ministered to us by works of fiction or of imaginative art, in which our own nature is set before us in more than human beauty and power. In truth, the soul is always bursting its limits. It thirsts continually for wider knowledge. It rushes forward to untried happiness. It has deep wants, which nothing limited can appease. Its true element and end is an unbounded good. Thus, God's infinity has its image in the soul; and through the soul, much more than through the universe, we arrive at this conception of the Deity.

In these remarks I have spoken strongly. But I have no fear of expressing too strongly the connection between the divine and the human mind. My only fear is that I shall dishonor the great subject. The danger to which we are most exposed is that of severing the Creator from his creatures. The propensity of human sovereigns to cut off communication between themselves and their subjects, and to disclaim a common nature with their inferiors, has led the multitude of men, who think of God chiefly under the character of a king, to conceive of him as a being who places his glory in multiplying distinctions between himself and all other beings. The truth is that the union between the Creator and the creature surpasses all other bonds in strength and intimacy. He penetrates all things, and delights to irradiate all with his glory. Nature, in all its lowest and inanimate forms, is pervaded by his power; and, when quickened by the mysterious property of life, how wonderfully does it show forth the perfections of its Author! How much of God may be seen in the structure of a single leaf, which, though so frail as to tremble in every wind, yet holds connections and living communications with the earth, the air, the clouds, and the distant sun, and, through these sympathies with the universe, is itself a revelation of an omnipotent mind! God delights to diffuse himself everywhere. Through his energy unconscious matter clothes itself with proportions, powers, and beauties which reflect his wisdom and love. How much more must He delight to frame conscious and happy recipients of his perfections, in whom his wisdom and love may substantially dwell, with whom He may form spiritual ties, and to whom He may be an everlasting spring of moral energy and happiness! How far the Supreme Being may communicate his attributes to his intelligent offspring, I stop not to inquire. But that his almighty goodness will impart to them powers and glories of which the material universe is but a faint emblem I cannot doubt. That the soul, if true to itself and its Maker, will be filled with God, and will manifest him more than the sun, I cannot doubt. Who can doubt it that believes and understands the doctrine of human immortality?

The views which I have given in this discourse respecting man's participation of the divine nature seem to me to receive strong confirmation from the title or relation most frequently applied to God in the New Testament; and I have reserved this as the last corroboration of this doctrine because, to my own mind, it is singularly affecting. In the New Testament God is made known to us as a Father; and a brighter feature of that book cannot be named. Our worship is to be directed to him as our Father. Our whole religion is to take its character from this view of the Divinity. In this He is to rise always to our minds. And what is it to be a father? It is to communicate one's own nature, to give life to kindred beings; and the highest function of a father is to educate the mind of the child, and to impart to it what is noblest and happiest in his own mind. God is our Father, not merely because He created us, or because He gives us enjoyment; for He created the flower and the insect, yet we call him not their Father. This bond is a spiritual one. This name belongs to God because He frames spirits like himself and delights to give them what is most glorious and blessed in his own nature. Accordingly, Christianity is said with special propriety to reveal God as the Father because it reveals him as sending his Son to cleanse the mind from every stain and to replenish it forever with the spirit and moral attributes of its Author. Separate from God this idea of his creating and training up beings after his own likeness, and you rob him of the paternal character. This relation vanishes, and with it vanishes the glory of the gospel and the dearest hopes of the human soul.

The greatest use which I would make of the principles laid down in this discourse is to derive from them just and clear views of the nature of religion. What, then, is religion? I answer, it is not the adoration of a God with whom we have no common properties, of a distinct, foreign, separate being, but of an all-communicating Parent. It recognizes and adores God as a being whom we know through our own souls; who has made man in his own image; who is the perfection of our own spiritual nature; who has sympathies with us as kindred beings; who is near us, not in place only like this all-surrounding atmosphere, but by spiritual influence and love;

who looks on us with parental interest, and whose great design it is to communicate to us forever, and in freer and fuller streams, his own power, goodness, and joy. The conviction of this near and ennobling relation of God to the soul, and of his great purposes toward it, belongs to the very essence of true religion; and true religion manifests itself chiefly and most conspicuously in desires, hopes, and efforts corresponding to this truth. It desires and seeks supremely the assimilation of the mind to God, or the perpetual unfolding and enlargement of those powers and virtues by which it is constituted his glorious image. The mind, in proportion as it is enlightened and penetrated by true religion, thirsts and labors for a god-like elevation. What else, indeed, can it seek if this good be placed within its reach? If I am capable of receiving and reflecting the intellectual and moral glory of my Creator, what else in comparison shall I desire? Shall I deem a property in the outward universe as the highest good when I may become partaker of the very mind from which it springs, of the prompting love, the disposing wisdom, the quickening power through which its order, beauty, and beneficent influences subsist? True religion is known by these high aspirations, hopes, and efforts. And this is the religion which most truly honors God. To honor him is not to tremble before him as an unapproachable sovereign, not to utter barren praise which leaves us as it found us. It is to become what we praise. It is to approach God as an inexhaustible fountain of light, power, and purity. It is to feel the quickening and transforming energy of his perfections. It is to thirst for the growth and invigoration of the divine principle within us. It is to seek the very spirit of God. It is to trust in, to bless, to thank him for that rich grace, mercy, love which was revealed and proffered by Jesus Christ, and which proposes as its great end the perfection of the human soul.

I regard this view of religion as infinitely important. It does more than all things to make our connection with our Creator ennobling and happy; and, in proportion as we want it, there is danger that the thought of God may itself become the instrument of our degradation. That religion has been so dispensed as to depress the human mind, I need not tell you; and it is a truth which ought to be known, that the greatness of the Deity, when separated in our thoughts from his parental character, especially tends to crush human energy and hope. To a frail, dependent creature, an omnipotent Creator easily becomes a terror, and his worship easily degenerates into servility, flattery, self-contempt, and selfish calculation. Religion only ennobles us in as far as it reveals to us the tender and intimate connection of God with his creatures, and teaches us to see in the very greatness which might give alarm the source of great and glorious communications to the human soul. You cannot, my hearers, think too highly of the majesty of God. But let not this majesty sever him from you. Remember that his greatness is the infinity of attributes which yourselves possess. Adore his infinite wisdom; but remember that this wisdom rejoices to diffuse itself, and let an exhilarating hope spring up at the thought of the immeasurable intelligence which such a Father must communicate to his children. In like manner adore his power. Let the boundless creation fill you with awe and admiration of the energy which sustains it. But remember that God has a nobler work than the outward creation, even the spirit within yourselves; and that it is his purpose to replenish this with his own energy, and to crown it with growing power and triumphs over the material universe. Above all, adore his unutterable goodness. But remember that this attribute is particularly proposed to you as your model; that God calls you, both by nature and revelation, to a fellowship in his philanthropy; that He has placed you in social relations for the very end of rendering you ministers and representatives of his benevolence; that He even summons you to espouse and to advance the sublimest purpose of his goodness, the redemption of the human race, by extending the knowledge and power of Christian truth. It is through such views that religion raises up the soul, and binds man by ennobling bonds to his Maker.

To complete my views of this topic, I beg to add an important caution. I have said that the great work of religion is to conform ourselves to God, or to unfold the divine likeness within us. Let none infer from this language that I place religion in unnatural effort, in straining after excitements which do not belong to the present state, or in anything separate from the clear and simple duties of life. I exhort you to no extravagance. I reverence human nature too much to do it violence. I see too much divinity in its ordinary operations to urge on it a forced and vehement virtue. To grow in the likeness of God we need not cease to be men. This likeness does not consist in extraordinary or miraculous gifts, in supernatural additions to the soul, or in anything foreign to our original constitution; but in our essential faculties, unfolded by vigorous and conscientious exertion in the ordinary circumstances assigned by God. To resemble our Creator we need not fly from society and entrance ourselves in lonely contemplation and prayer. Such processes might give a feverish strength to one class of emotions, but would result in disproportion, distortion, and sickliness of mind. Our proper work is to approach God by the free and natural unfolding of our highest powers—of understanding, conscience, love, and the moral will.

Shall I be told that, by such language, I ascribe to nature the effects which can only be wrought in the soul by the Holy Spirit? I anticipate this objection, and wish to meet it by a simple exposition of my views. I would on no account disparage the gracious aids and influences which God imparts to the human soul. The promise of the Holy Spirit is among the most precious in the Sacred Volume. Worlds could not tempt me to part with the doctrine of God's intimate connection with the mind, and of his free and full communications to it. But these views are in no respect at variance with what I have taught, of the method by which we are to grow in the likeness of God. Scripture and experience concur in teaching that, by the Holy Spirit, we are to understand a divine assistance adapted to our moral freedom and accordant with the fundamental truth that virtue is the mind's own work. By the Holy

Spirit, I understand an aid which must be gained and made effectual by our own activity; an aid which no more interferes with our faculties than the assistance which we receive from our fellow beings; an aid which silently mingles and conspires with all other helps and means of goodness; an aid by which we unfold our natural powers in a natural order, and by which we are strengthened to understand and apply the resources derived from our munificent Creator. This aid we cannot prize too much, or pray for too earnestly. But wherein, let me ask, does it war with the doctrine that God is to be approached by the exercise and unfolding of our highest powers and affections, in the ordinary circumstances of human life?

I repeat it, to resemble our Maker we need not quarrel with our nature or our lot. Our present state, made up as it is of aids and trials, is worthy of God, and may be used throughout to assimilate us to him. For example, our domestic ties, the relations of neighborhood and country, the daily interchanges of thoughts and feelings, the daily occasions of kindness, the daily claims of want and suffering—these and the other circumstances of our social state form the best sphere and school for that benevolence which is God's brightest attribute; and we should make a sad exchange by substituting for these natural aids any self-invented artificial means of sanctity. Christianity, our great guide to God, never leads us away from the path of nature, and never wars with the unsophisticated dictates of conscience. We approach our Creator by every right exertion of the powers He gives us. Whenever we invigorate the understanding by honestly and resolutely seeking truth, and by withstanding whatever might warp the judgment; whenever we invigorate the conscience by following it in opposition to the passions; whenever we receive a blessing gratefully, bear a trial patiently, or encounter peril or scorn with moral courage; whenever we perform a disinterested deed; whenever we lift up the heart in true adoration to God; whenever we war against a habit or desire which is strengthening itself against our higher principles; whenever we think, speak, or act with moral energy and resolute devotion to duty, be the occasion ever so humble, obscure, familiar—then the divinity is growing within us, and we are ascending toward our Author. True religion thus blends itself with common life. We are thus to draw nigh to God without forsaking men. We are thus, without parting with our human nature, to clothe ourselves with the divine.

My views on the great subject of this discourse have now been given. I shall close with a brief consideration of a few objections, in the course of which I shall offer some views of the Christian ministry which this occasion and the state of the world seem to me to demand. I anticipate from some an objection to this discourse, drawn as they will say from experience. I may be told that I have talked of the godlike capacities of human nature, and have spoken of man as a divinity; and where, it will be asked, are the warrants of this high estimate of our race? I may be told that I dream, and that I have peopled the world with the creatures of my lonely imagination. What! Is it only in dreams that beauty and loveliness have beamed on me from the human countenance, that I have heard tones of kindness which have thrilled through my heart, that I have found sympathy in suffering, and a sacred joy in friendship? Are all the great and good men of past ages only dreams? Are such names as Moses, Socrates, Paul, Alfred, Milton only the fictions of my disturbed slumbers? Are the great deeds of history, the discoveries of philosophy, the creations of genius, only visions? Oh, no. I do not dream when I speak of the divine capacities of human nature. It is a real page in which I read of patriots and martyrs, of Fénelon and Howard, of Hampden and Washington.[1] And tell me

---

[1] [François de Salignac de la Mothe Fénelon (1651-1715), French churchman and mystic whom Channing admired. See his "Remarks on the Character and Writings of Fénelon," *Works*, pp. 559-578.

[John Howard (1726-1790), English philanthropist and prison reformer.

[John Hampden (1595-1643), English statesman who played an influential role in resisting the crown's authority during the period before the Puritan revolution (1640-1644).]

not that these were prodigies, miracles, immeasurably separated from their race; for the very reverence which has treasured up and hallowed their memories, the very sentiments of admiration and love with which their names are now heard, show that the principles of their greatness are diffused through all your breasts. The germs of sublime virtue are scattered liberally on our earth. How often have I seen in the obscurity of domestic life a strength of love, of endurance, of pious trust, of virtuous resolution, which in a public sphere would have attracted public homage! I cannot but pity the man who recognizes nothing godlike in his own nature. I see the marks of God in the heavens and the earth, but how much more in a liberal intellect, in magnanimity, in unconquerable rectitude, in a philanthropy which forgives every wrong and which never despairs of the cause of Christ and human virtue! I do and I must reverence human nature. Neither the sneers of a worldly skepticism nor the groans of a gloomy theology disturb my faith in its godlike powers and tendencies. I know how it is despised, how it has been oppressed, how civil and religious establishments have for ages conspired to crush it. I know its history. I shut my eyes on none of its weaknesses and crimes. I understand the proofs by which despotism demonstrates that man is a wild beast, in want of a master, and only safe in chains. But injured, trampled on, and scorned as our nature is, I still turn to it with intense sympathy and strong hope. The signatures of its origin and its end are impressed too deeply to be ever wholly effaced. I bless it for its kind affections, for its strong and tender love. I honor it for its struggles against oppression, for its growth and progress under the weight of so many chains and prejudices, for its achievements in science and art, and still more for its examples of heroic and saintly virtue. These are marks of a divine origin and the pledges of a celestial inheritance; and I thank God that my own lot is bound up with that of the human race.

But another objection starts up. It may be said, "Allow these views to be true; are they fitted for the pulpit? Fitted to act on common minds? They may be prized by men of culti-

vated intellect and taste; but can the multitude understand
them? Will the multitude feel them? On whom has a minister
to act? On men immersed in business, and buried in the flesh;
on men whose whole power of thought has been spent on pleasure or gain; on men chained by habit and wedded to sin.
Sooner may adamant be riven by a child's touch than the human heart be pierced by refined and elevated sentiment.
Gross instruments will alone act on gross minds. Men sleep,
and nothing but thunder, nothing but flashes from the everlasting fire of hell, will thoroughly wake them."

I have all along felt that such objections would be made to
the views I have urged. But they do not move me. I answer
that I think these views singularly adapted to the pulpit, and I
think them full of power. The objection is that they are refined. But I see God accomplishing his noblest purposes by
what may be called refined means. All the great agents of nature—attraction, heat, and the principle of life—are refined,
spiritual, invisible, acting gently, silently, imperceptibly; and
yet brute matter feels their power, and is transformed by them
into surpassing beauty. The electric fluid, unseen, unfelt, and
everywhere diffused, is infinitely more efficient, and ministers
to infinitely nobler productions, than when it breaks forth in
thunder. Much less can I believe that in the moral world
noise, menace, and violent appeals to gross passions, to fear
and selfishness, are God's chosen means of calling forth spiritual life, beauty, and greatness. It is seldom that human nature throws off all susceptibility of grateful and generous impressions, all sympathy with superior virtue; and here are
springs and principles to which a generous teaching, if simple,
sincere, and fresh from the soul, may confidently appeal.

It is said men cannot understand the views which seem to
me so precious. This objection I am anxious to repel, for the
common intellect has been grievously kept down and wronged
through the belief of its incapacity. The pulpit would do
more good were not the mass of men looked upon and treated
as children. Happily for the race, the time is passing away in
which intellect was thought the monopoly of a few, and the

majority were given over to hopeless ignorance. Science is leaving her solitudes to enlighten the multitude. How much more may religious teachers take courage to speak to men on subjects which are nearer to them than the properties and laws of matter—I mean their own souls. The multitude, you say, want capacity to receive great truths relating to their spiritual nature. But what, let me ask you, is the Christian religion? A spiritual system, intended to turn men's minds upon themselves, to frame them to watchfulness over thought, imagination, and passion, to establish them in an intimacy with their own souls. What are all the Christian virtues which men are exhorted to love and seek? I answer, pure and high motions or determinations of the mind. That refinement of thought which, I am told, transcends the common intellect, belongs to the very essence of Christianity. In confirmation of these views, the human mind seems to me to be turning itself more and more inward, and to be growing more alive to its own worth and its capacities of progress. The spirit of education shows this, and so does the spirit of freedom. There is a spreading conviction that man was made for a higher purpose than to be a beast of burden or a creature of sense. The divinity is stirring within the human breast, and demanding a culture and a liberty worthy of the child of God. Let religious teaching correspond to this advancement of the mind. Let it rise above the technical, obscure, and frigid theology which has come down to us from times of ignorance, superstition, and slavery. Let it penetrate the human soul and reveal it to itself. No preaching, I believe, is so intelligible as that which is true to human nature and helps men to read their own spirits.

But the objection which I have stated not only represents men as incapable of understanding, but still more of being moved, quickened, sanctified, and saved by such views as I have given. If by this objection nothing more is meant than that these views are not alone or of themselves sufficient, I shall not dispute it; for, true and glorious as they are, they do not constitute the whole truth, and I do not expect great moral effects from narrow and partial views of our nature. I have spoken of the godlike capacities of the soul. But other and very different elements enter into the human being. Man has animal propensities as well as intellectual and moral powers. He has a body as well as mind. He has passions to war with reason, and self-love with conscience. He is a free being, and a tempted being, and thus constituted he may and does sin, and often sins grievously. To such a being religion, or virtue, is a conflict, requiring great spiritual effort, put forth in habitual watchfulness and prayer; and all the motives are needed by which force and constancy may be communicated to the will. I exhort not the preacher to talk perpetually of man as "made but a little lower than the angels." I would not narrow him to any class of topics. Let him adapt himself to our whole and various nature. Let him summon to his aid all the powers of this world and the world to come. Let him bring to bear on the conscience and the heart God's milder and more awful attributes, the promises and threatenings of the divine word, the lessons of history, the warnings of experience. Let the wages of sin here and hereafter be taught clearly and earnestly. But amidst the various motives to spiritual effort which belong to the minister, none are more quickening than those drawn from the soul itself, and from God's desire and purpose to exalt it by every aid consistent with its freedom. These views I conceive are to mix with all others, and without them all others fail to promote a generous virtue. Is it said that the minister's proper work is to preach Christ, and not the dignity of human nature? I answer that Christ's greatness is manifested in the greatness of the nature which he was sent to redeem; and that his chief glory consists in this, that he came to restore God's image where it was obscured or effaced, and to give an everlasting impulse and life to what is divine within us. Is it said that the malignity of sin is to be the minister's great theme? I answer that this malignity can only be understood and felt when sin is viewed as the ruin of God's noblest work, as darkening a light brighter than the sun, as carrying discord, bondage, disease, and death into a mind framed for perpetual progress toward its Author. Is it said that terror is the chief instrument of saving the soul? I answer that if by terror be meant a rational and moral fear, a conviction and dread of the unutterable evil incurred by a mind which wrongs, betrays, and destroys itself, then I am the last to deny its importance. But a fear like this, which regards the debasement of the soul as the greatest of evils, is plainly founded upon and proportioned to our conceptions of the greatness of our nature. The more common terror excited by vivid images of torture and bodily pain is a very questionable means of virtue. When strongly awakened, it generally injures the character, breaks men into cowards and slaves, brings the intellect to cringe before human authority, makes man abject before his Maker, and, by a natural reaction of the mind, often terminates in a presumptuous confidence altogether distinct from virtuous self-respect, and singularly hostile to the unassuming, charitable spirit of Christianity. The preacher should rather strive to fortify the soul against physical pains than to bow it to their mastery, teaching it to dread nothing in comparison with sin, and to dread sin as the ruin of a noble nature.

Men, I repeat it, are to be quickened and raised by appeals to their highest principles. Even the convicts of a prison may be touched by kindness, generosity, and especially by a tone, look, and address expressing hope and respect for their nature. I know that the doctrine of ages has been that terror, restraint, and bondage are the chief safeguards of human virtue and peace. But we have begun to learn that affection, confidence, respect, and freedom are mightier as well as nobler agents. Men can be wrought upon by generous influences. I would that this truth were better understood by religious teachers. From the pulpit generous influences too seldom proceed. In the church men too seldom hear a voice to quicken and exalt them. Religion, speaking through her public organs, seems often to forget her natural tone of elevation. The character of God, the principles of his government, his relations to the human family, the purposes for which He brought us into being, the nature which He has given us, and the condition in which

He has placed us—these and the like topics, though the sublimest which can enter the mind, are not unfrequently so set forth as to narrow and degrade the hearers, disheartening and oppressing with gloom the timid and sensitive, and infecting coarser minds with the unhallowed spirit of intolerance, presumption, and exclusive pretension to the favor of God. I know, and rejoice to know, that preaching in its worst forms does good; for so bright and piercing is the light of Christianity that it penetrates in a measure the thickest clouds in which men contrive to involve it. But that evil mixes with the good I also know; and I should be unfaithful to my deep convictions did I not say that human nature requires for its elevation more generous treatment from the teachers of religion.

I conclude with saying, Let the minister cherish a reverence for his own nature. Let him never despise it even in its most forbidding forms. Let him delight in its beautiful and lofty manifestations. Let him hold fast, as one of the great qualifications for his office, a faith in the greatness of the human soul —that faith which looks beneath the perishing body, beneath the sweat of the laborer, beneath the rags and ignorance of the poor, beneath the vices of the sensual and selfish, and discerns in the depths of the soul a divine principle, a ray of the Infinite Light, which may yet break forth and "shine as the sun" in the kingdom of God. Let him strive to awaken in men a consciousness of the heavenly treasure within them, a consciousness of possessing what is of more worth than the outward universe. Let hope give life to all his labors. Let him speak to men as to beings liberally gifted and made for God. Let him always look round on a congregation with the encouraging trust that he has hearers prepared to respond to the simple, unaffected utterance of great truths, and to the noblest workings of his own mind. Let him feel deeply for those in whom the divine nature is overwhelmed by the passions. Let him sympathize tenderly with those in whom it begins to struggle, to mourn for sin, to thirst for a new life. Let him guide and animate to higher and diviner virtue those in whom it has gained strength. Let him strive to infuse courage, enterprise, devout trust, and an inflexible will into men's labors for their own perfection. In one word, let him cherish an unfaltering and growing faith in God as the Father and quickener of the human mind, and in Christ as its triumphant and immortal friend. That by such preaching he is to work miracles, I do not say. That he will rival in sudden and outward effects what is wrought by the preachers of a low and terrifying theology, I do not expect or desire. That all will be made better, I am far from believing. His office is to act on free beings who, after all, must determine themselves; who have power to withstand all foreign agency; who are to be saved, not by mere preaching, but by their own prayers and toil. Still I believe that such a minister will be a benefactor beyond all praise to the human soul. I believe, and know, that on those who will admit his influence he will work deeply, powerfully, gloriously. His function is the sublimest under heaven; and his reward will be a growing power of spreading truth, virtue, moral strength, love, and happiness, without limit and without end.

HONOR DUE TO ALL MEN

1 Pet. ii. 17: "Honor all men."

Among the many and inestimable blessings of Christianity, I regard as not the least the new sentiment with which it teaches man to look upon his fellow beings; the new interest which it awakens in us toward everything human; the new importance which it gives to the soul; the new relation which it establishes between man and man. In this respect it began a mighty revolution, which has been silently spreading itself through society, and which, I believe, is not to stop until new ties shall have taken the place of those which have hitherto, in the main, connected the human race. Christianity has as yet but begun its work of reformation. Under its influences a new order of society is advancing, surely though slowly; and this beneficent change it is to accomplish in no small measure by revealing to men their own nature, and teaching them to "honor all" who partake it.

As yet Christianity has done little, compared with what it is to do, in establishing the true bond of union between man and man. The old bonds of society still continue in a great degree. They are instinct, interest, force. The true tie, which is mutual respect, calling forth mutual, growing, never-failing acts of love, is as yet little known. A new revelation, if I may so speak, remains to be made; or rather, the truths of the old revelation in regard to the greatness of human nature are to be brought out from obscurity and neglect. The soul is to be regarded with a religious reverence hitherto unfelt; and the solemn claims of every being to whom this divine principle is imparted are to be established on the ruins of those pernicious principles, both in church and state, which have so long divided mankind into the classes of the abject many and the self-exalting few.

There is nothing of which men know so little as themselves. They understand incomparably more of the surrounding creation, of matter and of its laws, than of that spiritual principle to which matter was made to be the minister, and without which the outward universe would be worthless. Of course, no man can be wholly a stranger to the soul, for the soul is himself, and he cannot but be conscious of its most obvious workings. But it is to most a chaos, a region shrouded in ever-shifting mists, baffling the eye and bewildering the imagination. The affinity of the mind with God, its moral power, the purposes for which its faculties were bestowed, its connection with futurity, and the dependence of its whole happiness on its own right action and progress—these truths, though they might be expected to absorb us, are to most men little more than sounds, and to none of us those living realities which, I trust, they are to become. That conviction, without which we are all poor, of the unlimited and immortal nature of the soul, remains in a great degree to be developed. Men have as yet no just respect for themselves, and of consequence no just respect for others. The true bond of society is thus wanting; and accordingly there is a great deficiency of Christian benevolence. There is, indeed, much instinctive, native benevolence, and this is not to be despised; but the benevolence of Jesus Christ, which consists in a calm purpose to suffer and, if need be, to die, for our fellow creatures, the benevolence of Christ on the cross, which is the true pattern to the Christian, this is little known; and what is the cause? It is this. We see nothing in human beings to entitle them to such sacrifices; we do not think them worth suffering for. Why should we be martyrs for beings who awaken in us little more of moral interest than the brutes?

I hold that nothing is to make man a true lover of man but the discovery of something interesting and great in human nature. We must see and feel that a human being is something important, and of immeasurable importance. We must see and feel the broad distance between the spiritual life within us and the vegetable or animal life which acts around us.

I cannot love the flower, however beautiful, with a disinterested affection which will make me sacrifice to it my own prosperity. You will in vain exhort me to attach myself, with my whole strength of affection, to the inferior animals, however useful or attractive; and why not? They want the capacity of truth, virtue, and progress. They want that principle of duty which alone gives permanence to a being; and accordingly they soon lose their individual nature, and go to mingle with the general mass. A human being deserves a different affection from what we bestow on inferior creatures, for he has a rational and moral nature by which he is to endure forever, by which he may achieve an unutterable happiness or sink into an unutterable woe. He is more interesting, through what is in him, than the earth or heavens; and the only way to love him aright is to catch some glimpse of this immortal power within him. Until this is done, all charity is little more than instinct; we shall embrace the great interests of human nature with coldness.

It may be said that Christianity has done much to awaken benevolence, and that it has taught men to call one another brethren. Yes, to *call* one another so; but has it as yet given the true feeling of brotherhood? We undoubtedly feel ourselves to be all of one race, and this is well. We trace ourselves up to one pair, and feel the same blood flowing in our veins. But do we understand our spiritual brotherhood? Do we feel ourselves to be derived from one Heavenly Parent, in whose image we are all made and whose perfection we may constantly approach? Do we feel that there is one divine life in our own and in all souls? This seems to me the only true bond of man to man. Here is a tie more sacred, more enduring, than all the ties of this earth. Is it felt, and do we in consequence truly honor one another?

Sometimes, indeed, we see men giving sincere, profound, and almost unmeasured respect to their fellow creatures; but to whom? To great men; to men distinguished by a broad line from the multitude; to men pre-eminent by genius, force of character, daring effort, high station, brilliant success. To such honor is given; but this is not to "honor all men"; and the homage paid to such is generally unfriendly to that Christian estimate of human beings for which I am now pleading. The great are honored at the expense of their race. They absorb and concentrate the world's admiration, and their less gifted fellow beings are thrown by their brightness into a deeper shade, and passed over with a colder contempt. Now I have no desire to derogate from the honor paid to great men, but I say, Let them not rise by the depression of the multitude. I say that great men, justly regarded, exalt our estimate of the human race and bind us to the multitude of men more closely; and when they are not so regarded, when they are converted into idols, when they serve to wean our interest from ordinary men, they corrupt us, they sever the sacred bond of humanity which should attach us to all, and our characters become vitiated by our very admiration of greatness. The true view of great men is that they are only examples and manifestations of our common nature, showing what belongs to all souls, though unfolded as yet only in a few. The light which shines from them is, after all, but a faint revelation of the power which is treasured up in every human being. They are not prodigies, not miracles, but natural developments of the human soul. They are indeed as men among children, but the children have a principle of growth which leads to manhood.

That great men and the multitude of minds are of one family is apparent, I think, in the admiration which the great inspire into the multitude. A sincere, enlightened admiration always springs from something congenial in him who feels it with him who inspires it. He that can understand and delight in greatness was created to partake of it; the germ is in him; and sometimes this admiration, in what we deem inferior minds, discovers a nobler spirit than belongs to the great man who awakens it; for sometimes the great man is so absorbed in his own greatness as to admire no other; and I should not hesitate to say that a common mind, which is yet capable of a generous admiration, is destined to rise higher than the man of eminent capacities who can enjoy no power or excellence but his own. When I hear of great men, I wish, not to separate them from their race, but to blend them with it. I esteem it no small benefit of the philosophy of mind that it teaches us that the elements of the greatest thoughts of the man of genius exist in his humbler brethren, and that the faculties which the scientific exert in the profoundest discoveries are precisely the same with those which common men employ in the daily labors of life.

To show the grounds on which the obligation to honor all men rests, I might take a minute survey of that human nature which is common to all, and set forth its claims to reverence. But, leaving this wide range, I observe that there is one principle of the soul which makes all men essentially equal, which places all on a level as to means of happiness, which may place in the first rank of human beings those who are the most depressed in worldly condition, and which therefore gives the most depressed a title to interest and respect. I refer to the sense of duty, to the power of discerning and doing right, to the moral and religious principle, to the inward monitor which speaks in the name of God, to the capacity of virtue or excellence. This is the great gift of God. We can conceive no greater. In seraph and archangel, we can conceive no higher energy than the power of virtue, or the power of forming themselves after the will and moral perfections of God. This power breaks down all barriers between the seraph and the lowest human being; it makes them brethren. Whoever has derived from God this perception and capacity of rectitude has a bond of union with the spiritual world stronger than all the ties of nature. He possesses a principle which, if he is faithful to it, must carry him forward forever, and insures to him the improvement and happiness of the highest order of beings.

It is this moral power which makes all men essentially equal, which annihilates all the distinctions of this world. Through this, the ignorant and the poor may become the greatest of the race; for the greatest is he who is most true to the principle of duty. It is not improbable that the noblest human beings are to be found in the least favored conditions of society, among those whose names are never uttered beyond the narrow circle in which they toil and suffer, who have but "two mites" to give away, who have perhaps not even that, but who "desire to be fed with the crumbs which fall from the rich man's table"; for in this class may be found those who have withstood the severest temptation, who have practiced the most arduous duties, who have confided in God under the heaviest trials, who have been most wronged and have forgiven most; and these are the great, the exalted. It matters nothing what the particular duties are to which the individual is called—how minute or obscure in their outward form. Greatness in God's sight lies, not in the extent of the sphere which is filled, or of the effect which is produced, but altogether in the power of virtue in the soul, in the energy with which God's will is chosen, with which trial is borne and goodness loved and pursued.

The sense of duty is the greatest gift of God. The idea of right is the primary and the highest revelation of God to the human mind, and all outward revelations are founded on and addressed to it. All mysteries of science and theology fade away before the grandeur of the simple perception of duty which dawns on the mind of the little child. That perception brings him into the moral kingdom of God. That lays on him an everlasting bond. He in whom the conviction of duty is unfolded becomes subject from that moment to a law which no power in the universe can abrogate. He forms a new and indissoluble connection with God, that of an accountable being. He begins to stand before an inward tribunal, on the decisions of which his whole happiness rests; he hears a voice which, if faithfully followed, will guide him to perfection, and in neglecting which he brings upon himself inevitable misery. We little understand the solemnity of the moral principle in every human mind. We think not how awful are its functions. We forget that it is the germ of immortality. Did we understand it, we should look with a feeling of reverence on every being to whom it is given.

Having shown, in the preceding remarks, that there is a foundation in the human soul for the honor enjoined in our text toward all men, I proceed to observe that, if we look next into Christianity, we shall find this duty enforced by new and still more solemn considerations. This whole religion is a testimony to the worth of man in the sight of God, to the importance of human nature, to the infinite purposes for which we were framed. God is there set forth as sending to the succor of his human family his Beloved Son, the bright image and representative of his own perfections; and sending him, not simply to roll away a burden of pain and punishment (for this, however magnified in systems of theology, is not his highest work), but to create men after that divine image which he himself bears, to purify the soul from every stain, to communicate to it new power over evil, and to open before it immortality as its aim and destination—immortality, by which we are to understand, not merely a perpetual, but an ever-improving and celestial being. Such are the views of Christianity. And these blessings it proffers, not to a few, not to the educated, not to the eminent, but to all human beings, to the poorest and the most fallen; and we know that, through the power of its promises, it has in not a few instances raised the most fallen to true greatness, and given them in their present virtue and peace an earnest of the Heaven which it unfolds. Such is Christianity. Men, viewed in the light of this religion, are beings cared for by God, to whom he has given his Son, on whom he pours forth his Spirit, and whom he has created for the highest good in the universe, for participation in his own perfections and happiness. My friends, such is Christianity. Our skepticism as to our own nature cannot quench the bright light which that religion sheds on the soul and on the prospects of mankind; and just as far as we receive its truth, we shall honor all men.

I know I shall be told that Christianity speaks of man as a

sinner, and thus points him out to abhorrence and scorn. I know it speaks of human sin, but it does not speak of this as indissolubly bound up with the soul, as entering into the essence of human nature, but as a temporary stain, which it calls on us to wash away. Its greatest doctrine is that the most lost are recoverable, that the most fallen may rise, and that there is no height of purity, power, felicity in the universe to which the guiltiest mind may not, through penitence, attain. Christianity, indeed, gives us a deeper, keener feeling of the guilt of mankind than any other religion. By the revelation of perfection in the character of Jesus Christ, it shows us how imperfect even the best men are. But it reveals perfection in Jesus, not for our discouragement, but as our model—reveals it only that we may thirst for and approach it. From Jesus I learn what man is to become, that is, if true to this new light; and true he may be.

Christianity, I have said, shows man as a sinner, but I nowhere meet in it those dark views of our race which would make us shrink from it as from a nest of venomous reptiles. According to the courteous style of theology, man has been called half brute and half devil. But this is a perverse and pernicious exaggeration. The brute, as it is called—that is, animal—appetite is indeed strong in human beings; but is there nothing within us but appetite? Is there nothing to war with it? Does this constitute the essence of the soul? Is it not rather an accident, the result of the mind's union with matter? Is not its spring in the body, and may it not be expected to perish with the body? In addition to animal propensities, I see the tendency to criminal excess in all men's passions. I see not one only, but many tempters in every human heart. Nor am I insensible to the fearful power of these enemies to our virtue. But is there nothing in man but temptation, but propensity to sin? Are there no counterworking powers? no attractions in virtue? no tendencies to God? no sympathies with sorrow? no reverence for greatness? no moral conflicts? no triumphs of principle? This very strength of temptation seems to me to be one of the indications of man's greatness. It shows a being framed to make progress through difficulty, suffering, and conflict; that is, it shows a being designed for the highest order of virtues; for we all feel by an unerring instinct that virtue is elevated in proportion to the obstacles which it surmounts, to the power with which it is chosen and held fast. I see men placed by their Creator on a field of battle, but compassed with peril that they may triumph over it; and, though often overborne, still summoned to new efforts, still privileged to approach the Source of all Power and to seek "grace in time of need," and still addressed in tones of encouragement by a celestial Leader who has himself fought and conquered and holds forth to them his own crown of righteousness and victory.

From these brief views of human nature and of Christianity, you will see the grounds of the solemn obligation of honoring all men, of attaching infinite importance to human nature, and of respecting it, even in its present infant, feeble, tottering state. This sentiment of honor or respect for human beings strikes me more and more as essential to the Christian character. I conceive that a more thorough understanding and a more faithful culture of this would do very much to carry forward the church and the world. In truth, I attach to this sentiment such importance that I measure by its progress the progress of society. I judge of public events very much by their bearing on this. I estimate political revolutions chiefly by their tendency to exalt men's conceptions of their nature and to inspire them with respect for one another's claims. The present stupendous movements in Europe naturally suggest, and almost force upon me, this illustration of the importance which I have given to the sentiment enjoined in our text. Allow me to detain you a few moments on this topic.[1]

What is it, then, I ask, which makes the present revolu-

1 [Channing refers to the revolutionary movement which, beginning in 1830 with the overthrow of Charles X in France, spread throughout Europe in the succeeding months. With but few exceptions, the varied political and nationalist aspirations of the revolutionaries were eventually defeated. In England, the movement manifested itself in the social and political agitation which culminated in the passage of the Reform Act of 1832.]

tionary movement abroad so interesting? I answer that I see in it the principle of respect for human nature and for the human race developing itself more powerfully, and this to me constitutes its chief interest. I see in it proofs, indications, that the mind is awakening to a consciousness of what it is and of what it is made for. In this movement I see man becoming to himself a higher object. I see him attaining to the conviction of the equal and indestructible rights of every human being. I see the dawning of that great principle, that the individual is not made to be the instrument of others but to govern himself by an inward law and to advance toward his proper perfection; that he belongs to himself and to God, and to no human superior. I know, indeed, that in the present state of the world these conceptions are exceedingly unsettled and obscure; and, in truth, little effort has hitherto been made to place them in a clear light and to give them a definite and practical form in men's minds. The multitude know not with any distinctness what they want. Imagination, unschooled by reason and experience, dazzles them with bright but baseless visions. They are driven onward with a perilous violence by a vague consciousness of not having found their element; by a vague yet noble faith in a higher good than they have attained; by impatience under restraints which they feel to be degrading. In this violence, however, there is nothing strange, nor ought it to discourage us. It is, I believe, universally true that great principles, in their first development, manifest themselves irregularly. It is so in religion. In history we often see religion, especially after long depression, breaking out in vehemence and enthusiasm, sometimes stirring up bloody conflicts, and through struggles establishing a calmer empire over society. In like manner, political history shows us that men's consciousness of their rights and essential equality has at first developed itself passionately. Still the consciousness is a noble one, and the presage of a better social state.

Am I asked what I hope from the present revolutionary movements in Europe? I answer that I hope a good which includes all others, and which almost hides all others from my view. I hope the subversion of institutions by which the true bond between man and man has been more or less dissolved, by which the will of one or a few has broken down the will, the heart, the conscience of the many; and I hope that in the place of these are to grow up institutions which will express, cherish, and spread far and wide a just respect for human nature, which will strengthen in men a consciousness of their powers, duties, and rights, which will train the individual to moral and religious independence, which will propose as their end the elevation of all orders of the community, and which will give full scope to the best minds in this work of general improvement. I do not say that I expect it to be suddenly realized. The sun, which is to bring on a brighter day, is rising in thick and threatening clouds. Perhaps the minds of men were never more unquiet than at the present moment. Still I do not despair. That a higher order of ideas or principles is beginning to be unfolded; that a wider philanthropy is beginning to triumph over the distinctions of ranks and nations; that a new feeling of what is due to the ignorant, poor, and depraved has sprung up; that the right of every human being to such an education as shall call forth his best faculties, and train him more and more to control himself, is recognized as it never was before; and that government is more and more regarded as intended, not to elevate the few, but to guard the rights of all; that these great revolutions in principle have commenced and are spreading, who can deny? And to me they are prophetic of an improved condition of human nature and human affairs. Oh, that this melioration might be accomplished without blood! As a Christian, I feel a misgiving when I rejoice in any good, however great, for which this fearful price has been paid. In truth, a good so won is necessarily imperfect and generally transient. War may subvert a despotism but seldom builds up better institutions. Even when joined, as in our own history, with high principles, it inflames and leaves behind it passions which make liberty a feverish conflict of jealous parties, and which expose a people to the tyranny of faction under the forms of freedom. Few things impair men's reverence for human nature more than war; and did I not see other and holier influences than the sword working out the regeneration of the race, I should indeed despair.

In this discourse I have spoken of the grounds and importance of that honor or respect which is due from us, and enjoined on us, toward all human beings. The various forms in which this principle is to be exercised or manifested I want time to enlarge on. I would only say, "Honor all men." Honor man, from the beginning to the end of his earthly course. Honor the child. Welcome into being the infant with a feeling of its mysterious grandeur, with the feeling that an immortal existence has begun, that a spirit has been kindled which is never to be quenched. Honor the child. On this principle all good education rests. Never shall we learn to train up the child till we take it in our arms, as Jesus did, and feel distinctly that "of such is the kingdom of heaven." In that short sentence is taught the spirit of the true system of education; and for want of understanding it, little effectual aid, I fear, is yet given to the heavenly principle in the infant soul. —Again. Honor the poor. This sentiment of respect is essential to improving the connection between the more and less prosperous conditions of society. This alone makes beneficence truly godlike. Without it, almsgiving degrades the receiver. We must learn how slight and shadowy are the distinctions between us and the poor; and that the last in outward condition may be first in the best attributes of humanity. A fraternal union, founded on this deep conviction and intended to lift up and strengthen the exposed and tempted poor, is to do infinitely more for that suffering class than all our artificial associations; and till Christianity shall have breathed into us this spirit of respect for our nature, wherever it is found, we shall do them little good. I conceive that, in the present low state of Christian virtue, we little apprehend the power which might be exerted over the fallen and destitute by a benevolence which should truly, thoroughly recognize in them the image of God.

Perhaps none of us have yet heard or can comprehend the tone of voice in which a man, thoroughly impressed with this sentiment, would speak to a fellow creature. It is a language hardly known on earth; and no eloquence, I believe, has achieved such wonders as it is destined to accomplish. I must stop, though I have but begun the application of the principle which I have urged. I will close as I began, with saying that the great revelation which man now needs is a revelation of man to himself. The faith which is most wanted is a faith in what we and our fellow beings may become—a faith in the divine germ or principle in every soul. In regard to most of what are called the mysteries of religion, we may innocently be ignorant. But the mystery within ourselves, the mystery of our spiritual, accountable, immortal nature, it behooves us to explore. Happy are they who have begun to penetrate it, and in whom it has awakened feelings of awe toward themselves, and of deep interest and honor toward their fellow creatures.